George Dana Mumford

THE
AYAR-INCAS

"MANCO CCAPAC"

*From "Monarquia Peruana," by Dr. Justo Sa-
huaraura, Inca.*

Designated by Blas Valera as Ayar Manco. Eighty-sixth king from Pirua Paccari Manco. Ayar Manco reestablished the Ayar rule in Cuzco after the exile in Tampu-tocco. The personal appearance and regalia of the various Incas were represented in: 1.—Pictures hung on the walls of the lineal descendant of the Inca Emperors, Dr. Pablo Justiniani, at Laris; 2.—Pictures sketched by Don Felipe Huaman Poma de Ayala, Chief of Lucanas,—whose "mother was a daughter of the great Inca, Tupac Yupanqui"; 3.—Pictures of the Incas sent by their descendants in Peru in 1603 to Garcilasso de la Vega, Alonzo de Mesa, and Melchior Carlos Inca in Spain,—their representatives before the Spanish crown, in their effort to recover some of their property and privileges. These remaining Incas in Peru (SIR CLEMENTS R. MARKHAM, *Incas of Peru,* 281) "sent proofs of their descent painted on a yard and a half of white silk of China with the Incas in their ancient dresses."

THE
AYAR-INCAS

By

MILES POINDEXTER, LL.D.,

FORMER UNITED STATES SENATOR.
LATE AMBASSADOR TO PERU. F.R.G.S., ETC.

VOLUME ONE

Monuments, Culture, and American Relationships

"En remontant dans les tables chronologiques des Mexicains, par les périodes de treize en treize ans, on trouve marqué à un signe *Ce-Tecpatl*, Un silex, le récit encore fort obscur du voyage des *Chichimeques* au pays de *Tlapallan*, Terre Colorée, ou *Hue-hue-Tlapallan*, Terre Colorée des Anciens."

BRASSEUR DE BOURBOURG, *Popol Vuh*, LXIII.

1930
HORACE LIVERIGHT . NEW YORK

PRINTED IN THE U. S. A. BY
QUINN & BODEN COMPANY, INC.
RAHWAY, N. J.

To My Mother

JOSEPHINE ANDERSON POINDEXTER

AMID GREAT TRIALS SHE MAINTAINED
HER SOUL IN DAUNTLESS COURAGE AND
PLANTED THE PRECIOUS SEED OF HER DE-
VOTION.   IN THE SWIFT ACCUMULATION
OF THE YEARS HER MEMORY GROWS MORE
LUXURIANTLY.

"They that sow in tears shall reap in joy.
"He that goeth forth and weepeth, bearing precious
seed, shall doubtless come again with rejoicing, bringing
his sheaves with him."

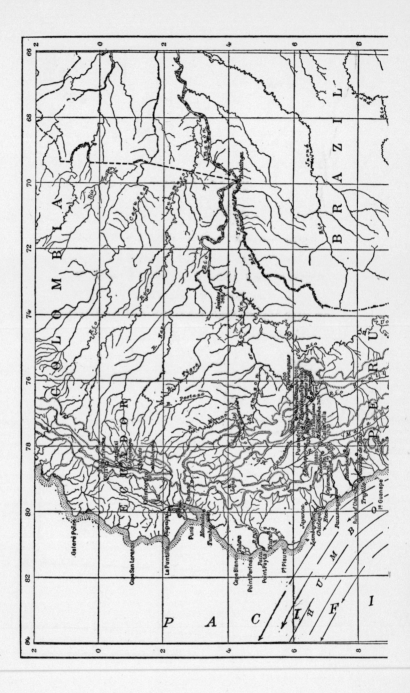

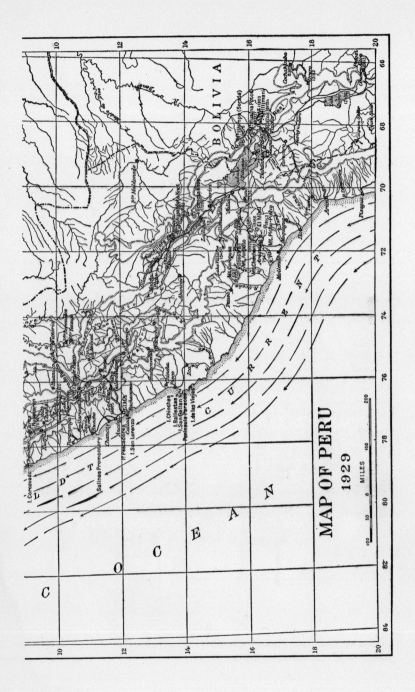

MAP OF PERU
1929

ACKNOWLEDGMENT

THE author takes this means of expressing his thanks to the Geographic Society of Lima for valuable information furnished him at various times and especially for a complete set of the very valuable *Boletines* of that Society; to the *Biblioteca Nacional* of Lima for the free use of its library and for the loan of books; to Mr. H. Hope-Jones for data furnished by him; to Bertram T. Lee, Esq., of Lima, for valuable documents and much valuable information (Mr. Lee is referred to in other volumes on Peru); to the American Geographical Society for the preparation of maps; to His Excellency, President Augusto B. Leguía, and to the Peruvian officials and people generally for their unfailing hospitality and many kindnesses during my residence and travels in their country, where, due to their friendship, I came to feel very much at home.

Especially I express my deep appreciation to Miss Harriett E. Meek for her invaluable aid in typing my confused and almost illegible manuscripts.

MILES POINDEXTER.

Lima, Peru,
March 1, 1928.

PREFACE TO VOLUME ONE

By a strange bent archæologists have been accustomed to give but small consideration to the sea in tracing ancient migrations. Most of the great human settlements are on the sea. Most of the great commercial capitals of the modern world trace their foundations back to very early historic—some of them to prehistoric—time. They owe their location to the fact that they are on, or easily accessible to, the great highways of the ocean. This is an outstanding proof that in those early times man's chief road was the sea.

As one looks out upon the sea from the deck of a ship plowing along a route of modern commerce and travel,—the curving watery expanse flecked with sun and shadows, rippling in the trade wind,—it does not seem a "gray and melancholy waste," but a cheerful and hospitable highway, teeming with life, stretching away into immeasurable distances, traversable by a good boat, even though it be a small one, manned by a competent navigator, to all the principal marts and meetings points of men.

This highway leads to most of the centers of culture of ancient and modern times. Man learned to travel it in a very early stage of his development. Its route along the coast from headland to headland, from Mexico to Peru, or from island to island across the benign Pacific, must be taken as the principal factor in solving the problem of the early cultures of America.

In the Pleistocene age man followed the animals on which he fed across Bering Strait (or where the strait now is) and pushed on to most parts of the two continents. Many thousands of years later, and in various epochs, new infusions of different races came by the islands of the Pacific,—some pushing along the north Asiatic coast and in slow stages following the Aleutian chain,—carrying their primitive culture thence both to the south along the coast of Alaska, and eastward on the fierce but fecund archipelagos of the Arctic as far east as Greenland.

In both early and later times there were bolder ventures of a greater race by the chains of islands and across the great intervening spaces of the central and south Pacific to the shores of Mexico and Peru. Mixed races came, the black Melanesian and the white Proto-Aryan. The Inca Tupac carried an army in a fleet of canoes and balsas from the mainland of South America to the Galápagos Islands and found there black men, some of whom he brought back with him on his return to Peru. Mrs. Scoresby Routledge was surprised to find strong traces of Melanesian blood in the present inhabitants of Easter Island.

There was an age of great navigators in Polynesia who found their way across the intervening two thousand miles from Tahiti to Hawaii; also to the Paumotus, to Easter Island, and to the mainland of America. They made their voyages in vessels that were as large as some of those in which Columbus, Cook, and Magellan, as well as the great Dutch and French navigators, accomplished their marvelous explorations, and much larger than those with which Captain Slocum and other daring sailors have sailed around the world for sport in recent years—huge "dug-outs" built up on the sides, double, with a connecting framework, raised-deck platforms and sheltered cabins, propelled by sails and paddles.

When the earliest European navigators reached the Pacific islands *they found white men there*, chiefly a ruling caste governing the darker peoples. These were descend-ants of the white Aryan or Proto-Aryan archaic stock, whose kinsmen erected the megaliths of Easter Island and carried the art of their masonry to Peru.

In prehistoric America the struggle of this white race of rulers to preserve the purity of its blood in the midst of a mass of "darker peoples," was carried on just as it had been in Asia, especially in India, and also in Poly-nesia, by a system of caste and with the same result—the gradual victory of the indomitable appeal of sex, the losing struggle of the priestly and kingly caste to preserve the purity of their race, the absorption of the smaller white element in the tide of darker blood.

The eastward-moving branch of the forefathers of the white race reached America and established the typical culture of the white Proto-Aryan peoples in America before their westward-moving archaic kinsmen had car-ried their religion and arts to Europe.

Civilizations which were refined in some respects, crude and gross in others, were developed in Peru and Mexico under the leadership of this white race,—or so much of it as had survived,—before Europe had emerged from absolute barbarism.

From these foundations distinct and indigenous cultures were evolved in the fertile environments of America; and to this present day, even after the wreck of the Spanish conquest, there may be found among the remnants of the early peoples, especially in the isolated villages of the Andes, marked traces of the blood, language, and religion which we ourselves have inherited by way of Europe from the same archaic Asiatic source. Striking evidences of this are set out in this work.

In Peru the conception of God as an invisible and omnipotent spirit—a conception which had been attained by the ruling Ayar caste—was as refined and exalted as our own. It had been evolved in the same way from the same source. The Peruvian Ayars worshipped God with much the same prayers as we repeat today from our prayer book and sung to Him the same pæans of praise as have come down to us in the Psalms of David. They carried in their journey to the Peruvian Holy Land—the "Sacred Valley" of the Vilcanota—the same type of ark containing a mystic and divine manifestation as was carried by the Israelites in the wilderness and as was common to many early religions of the east.

Especially the arts of weaving and of masonry, both of which have been potent and characteristic factors in the progress of Aryan culture, were carried to a higher degree of excellence, merely as such, in Peru than they have attained even in our present industrial age, or in the marvelous Renaissance of Europe, or in the ancient civilizations of Asia and the Mediterranean.

A great mass of our own most intimate words, redolent of pre-Aryan Asiatic origins, naming the essential and simple contacts of daily life, in common use by us today, were also used by our pre-Columbian kinsmen in Central America, Mexico, and Peru.

The religion and art of the various American peoples had been affected and modified in the long ages of its evolution in America by many things besides environment, profound as was the influence of the tremendous geographical features and phenomena of the vast American continents. Commerce was actively carried on between North and South America long before the arrival of the Spaniards.

Mayan place-names are common in the Peruvian highlands and the name of the great *Quiché* race and culture of Guatemala is preserved to this day in that of the Quichua (Quiché),—the basic stock of the Peruvian Andes over whom the noble caste of Ayars (Aryas), ancestors and forerunners of the Incas, established their rule. The Quichua today (the related peoples so called from the name of one of the early tribes) constitutes approximately 85% of the population of Peru. The relation of the Quichés to the Toltecs and other Anahuac races of the Mexican tableland is thoroughly recognized.

Elements of Mexican culture had been carried by sea across the Gulf of Mexico, both to the Antilles and to the mainland of what is now the southern United States, but its principal migrations were to the south. Mexican corn had been carried to Peru but the Peruvian potato had not been brought to Mexico.

In the mixture of races and influences the Atlantic had also had its part. Long before Columbus, white men from Europe, passing by way of the chain of islands bordering the Arctic, had established colonies in America. These had disappeared but had undoubtedly left the influences of their race and religion. There were before Columbus unmistakable traces of African contact on the east coast of South America.[1]

The American race before Columbus was not a fixed and single racial type; nor was its culture a stereotyped form from any one single source. Both race and culture

[1] *Africa and the Discovery of America.* Leo Wiener. The persistent stories of the "Western Islands" in the Atlantic (St. Brendan's, Atlantis, etc.) while vague and somewhat mythical were probably based on traditions of actual lands in the west (islands or portions of the continent of America), of which reports had come in very early times in various ways. "In *1463* a map by Benincasa indicated at a great distance from Europe the island of Antille of great extent,—also the island of Salvaga, and even still further off (towards the west) the island of Roselia." *Geographic Knowledge of the Atlantic in the Time of Christopher Columbus* by A. Hautreux, translated from the *Bulletin de la Societé de Geographie Commerciale* de Bordeaux by C. J. B. *Bol. Soc. Geog. de Lima*, Tom. II, Año II, p. 207, Lima, 1893.

On his second voyage Columbus found the wreck of a European-built ship on the beach of Guadeloupe. (*The American Indian* by A. H. Verrill, p. 4.)

None of these circumstances, however, detract in the slightest degree from the fame and credit of Columbus for his greatest of all discoveries, any more than the fact that this western world when discovered was found to be already inhabited by a more or less cultured race which drew the best of its culture from the same archaic sources which had supplied the "Promethean Fire" to Europe. However many times it had been visited by Asiatics, Africans, or Europeans, it was as absolutely unknown to the active world of Europe of Columbus' day as though it had never been trodden by the foot of man.

Europe's ignorance of America was only a part of its *general* provincialism. Even yet the world still remains unacquainted with brilliant cultures of which it is only beginning to discover the vestiges.

Just as the ignorance of previous geographical discoveries of America in Columbus' day,—the present lack of knowledge of the contact of Asia with ancient American civilizations is only illustrative of the meagerness of information and apparent total misconception of early cultures in general,—not only those of America and Asia but of Europe itself. (*Downland Man*, by H. J. Massingham.) The impetus which nerved Columbus to his immortal achievement was the general revival of learning,—the intellectual Renaissance.

were mixed from many sources and both were under-
going constant changes. America itself, though unknown
to the Europe of that day, was not unknown to nor out
of contact with Asia in early times. Life in America
before Columbus was not a deadly isolation from the rest
of the world nor a paralyzing provincialism within itself.

There was the stimulus of frequent new infusions, both
from Asia by way of Bering Sea and the southern islands
and ocean currents, and less influential and less frequent
contacts of both white and black men from beyond the
Atlantic; almost constant exchanges of commerce and culture carried on in picturesque voyages along the coast,—
explorations and migrations, both by sea and land, in both
North and South America,—which provided impulse and
variety. There was food for the imagination. It was
no pent-up and solitary tribe but a boundless and active
world in which the cultures of America were evolved.

The great age of enterprise in the Pacific had passed
long before Columbus. The race of adventurous and
able navigators who had colonized Hawaii, Easter Island,
and the widely separated archipelagos of Polynesia,
seemed to be extinct or in decay. Probably this decadence
was due to the absorption of the racial strain by inferior
peoples; the amalgamation of the great white Caucasian
or Proto-Aryan—Polynesian stock with the Melanesian or
other darker peoples.

The same process had taken place on the continents of
Asia and America. The age of the megalithic builders
and the megalithic masonry of Peru had passed before the
arrival of the Spaniards. It had passed so long ago that
the mighty race which achieved these wonderful works

was lost to all but the traditions—and lost even to the traditions except in a vague and uncertain style—of the Ayar-Inca and Quichua people of Peru at the time of the Conquest.

The white race itself had been absorbed in the mass of the darker indigenous people. However, its monuments and much of its culture and, in the high Andes and in the upper castes, even something of its lighter color had survived.[2] The uncultivated tribes who inhabited America at the time of Columbus' discovery of the continent were not in all cases a savage people working up from a lower condition; but in many instances they were the decadent remnants of a former cultured race.

This is not a *history* of the Incas. Insofar as their history is known, it has been often written; and while a compilation and restatement of what is known or conjectured of the line of ancient Peruvian Kings and the race from which they sprang would be interesting, it is only incidentally and in certain aspects within the scope of this work. The comments contained in these volumes deal rather with origins and relations (some of them of course merely hypothetical),—and even as to these only in certain phases.

What has been written here by no means purports to be a complete archæological or technical ethnological

[2] "Many generations of culture and of rule had produced men of a very different type from any Peruvian-Indian of today. We see the Incas in the pictures of the church of Santa Ana at Cuzco. The color of the skin was many shades lighter than that of the downtrodden descendants of their subjects; the forehead high, the nose slightly aquiline, the chin and the mouth firm, the whole face majestic, refined, and intellectual." Sir Clements R. Markham, *Incas of Peru*, page 12.

treatment of the subject. Certain features only of these which appear interesting in themselves and which bear directly upon the suggestions of the origins of this interesting race are discussed and these necessarily in limited fields.

Many of the megalithic and other monuments (temples, palaces, altars, and fortresses) partially described in the work have often been written about before. The purpose in mentioning them here is to record a new viewpoint and a somewhat different impression of their purpose and significance.

The view expressed here of the *Ayar-Incas* is not the conventional view. In fact in some respects it is even opposed to the conventional view and as such of course invites criticism. However, even where there is disagreement, opinions, based upon years of study and personal observation, tend to elucidation of the truth and are convincing only to the extent that they are supported by reason and proof. The very title of this work itself, in the emphasis that it gives to the name of *Ayar*, suggests a new conception of the *Incas*.

MILES POINDEXTER.

Lima, Peru,
March 1, 1928.

CONTENTS—VOLUME ONE

xix

ILLUSTRATIONS—VOLUME ONE

THE AYAR-INCAS

VOLUME ONE

Monuments, Culture, and American Relationships

REMAINS OF INCA ROAD

Steps cut in natural rock, worn smooth by travel. Valley of the Vilcanota.

Photograph by the author.

I

THE BATTLE-GAP

FROM the north end of Lake Titicaca the pampa,—covered in the spring with flowers like our western prairies, brown and sear in the winter,—rises towards the converging mountains to the north. At first a steady although almost imperceptible grade, it steepens towards the summit, to a height of 1618 feet above the level of the lake, at the pass of the Vilcanota ninety-nine miles north.

Many authors speak of the apparent marvel that a race sufficiently numerous to have erected the megalithic structures of Tiahuanaco could have been supported on the high and comparatively barren soil of the basin of Lake Titicaca. As a matter of fact a large population of Aymará Indians,—and about the north end of the lake some Quichuas,—descendants of the ancient peoples, is supported there today entirely on the resources of the country under far less advantageous economic conditions of government, organization, and culture than in the ancient times. The altitude of the lake is 12,500 feet, and, to those who are adapted to it, the climate of the region is wholesome and invigorating.

The ancient inhabitants of the Titicaca basin were largely herdsmen, as they are today.[1] Nutritious grasses

[1] *Quichua* is probably based on the root *ichu,*—the coarse grass of the mountain ranges,—and means dwellers in the grass country, or herdsmen. The Andes from above the line of the western desert to the snow line, and on the eastern slopes to the borders of the tropical forests in the foothills,

of several kinds grow luxuriantly in the valleys of the thirty rivers flowing from the surrounding cordilleras into the lake on all sides,—and on the slopes of the higher mountains up to the snow-line,—and in the ancient days furnished pasturage for vast herds of llamas and alpacas. Much of the land, especially the alluvial soil in the innumerable coulees and on the creek borders, is extremely fertile, and potatoes, oca, and other tubers, beans, quinoa, and even a diminutive maize flourish and mature there. Barley is also raised for forage but does not ripen in the grain.

The great range of the *Andes,*—meaning in Quichua "the front range" [2] or specifically "that range of the vast system of the cordilleras which fronts the ocean,"—enclosing on the west with its mighty barricade of sierras and snow-peaks the great basin of Titicaca, after passing the northern end of the beautiful lake veers to the east and forms a junction with the central range of the great mountain system. Many of the old Spanish geographers called this central range *The Cordillera,* by way of distinction from the Andes proper.[3]

The great mass of snowy mountains, the section of the central cordillera lying southeast of Lake Titicaca, is called the Cordillera Real. Its line of seventy-five miles of unbroken snow and glacier fields encloses the water-

are a vast treeless grass-covered pasture. (Note the Quiché *ichah,* edible plants. Bourbourg.) Aymará, the name of the closely related neighboring race, seems to be derived from a root word meaning *crop,* or *to harvest,*— and probably was suggested by the occupation of these people as farmers. Markham (*Incas of Peru,* Appendix B) gives his analysis of the extension of these names from the original tribes, so called, to include many other tribes.

[2] Fidel Lopez, *Les Races Aryennes du Pérou,* p. 348.

[3] Of course the whole system is now included under the name Andes.

shed of Titicaca on the southeast and feeds from its
immense eastern slope the myriad streams which form
the Beni,—gigantic tributary of the Madeira. A hundred
miles north of Lake Titicaca the two great cordilleras

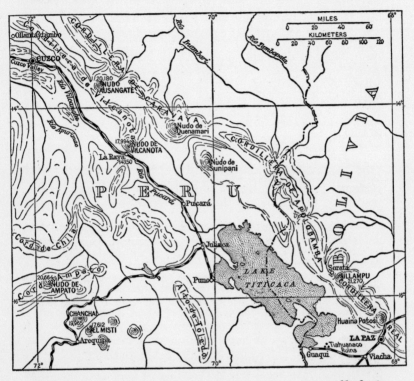

merge for a short distance in the huge mass called the
"Knot" of Vilcanota and enclose, on that side, the vast
watershed of Titicaca, whose waters flow without other
outlet into the shallow mountain lagoon of Poopo and
the extensive salt marshes of southern Bolivia. In this
great enclosed basin to the south of Lake Titicaca the
pampa leads between the cordilleras to the plains whence

came the hordes [4] of the Argentine and Chile. It is the primeval highway of races.

Up this highway came the invaders from the south, so constantly though vaguely referred to in the Inca traditions,—to attack and overthrow the ancient civilization of Tiahuanaco and that of the still richer and more inviting valley of the Vilcanota with its megalithic capital of Cuzco. No doubt earlier leaders, bringing the primitive early Aryan culture from the islands in the west,—who had been carried by the currents of the ocean on to the continental coast further south,[5]—had also penetrated inland from the desert shore. They came possibly up the

[4] The tradition of the Ayars was that the tribes who attacked them in the pass of Vilcanota, and who finally carried that stronghold and overthrew the Ayar rule, came from the south. These hordes from the southern plains no doubt came by the great thoroughfare of the intercordilleran pampa.

[5] It is an interesting circumstance that the seed-bearing cones of the Araucaria fir were apparently carried by the great South Pacific current,—which divides on the southern point of the continent,—from New Zealand to Chile and Brazil.

The Polynesian immigrants left a record of their settlement on the coast in the name of *Arica* (quite well known as the subject of dispute between Chile and Peru). The railroad from this port to La Paz follows the probable trail of the ancient immigrants up the *quebrada* (cañon) of a small river to the great inter-cordilleran pampa and the valley of Lake Titicaca.

Ariki was the title of the Polynesian High Chief,—the Highest Born, the chief descendant of the chief ancestor. (Hare Rongi, *Polyn. Soc. Jour.*, XVIII, 84.) The meaning of Ari'i (or Ariki) is chief, or head chief. (Tati Salmon, *Polyn. Soc. Jour.*, XIX, 39.) *Infra*, pp. 131, n. 14; 154, 167.

In some of the Polynesian islands Ariki was the title of the High Priest.

The ancient village of Arica is at the point where the shore-line of the continent makes its great bulge to the west and where voyagers on the great South Pacific current, which strikes here in full force, would be naturally brought to land.

Ari, Cari, are given as forms of the same title of Ariki. These names appear in the records and traditions as the names or titles of white leaders in localities as far apart as the Polynesian islands, Florida, and Lake Titicaca. The title appears in the names of several of the Ayar-Amauta kings of Cuzco.

valleys of some of the rivers, found their way to the high pampa and followed this broad primeval highway to the north to establish their culture at Tiahuanaco.

Tradition locates on an island in Lake Titicaca the "first civilizers,—white, bearded men." Cieza de Leon speaks of "white people, with beards, who lived on the larger island of the lake . . . before the reign of the Incas." [6] "Their Captain, who was named Cari, arrived at the place where Chucuito now stands, whence after having founded some new settlements, he passed over with his people to the island. He made such war upon the inhabitants that he killed them all." [7]

This same name Cari, or Cauri, descended to the Amauta line, predecessors and ancestors of the Incas, and appears also in the name of Tupac Cauri,[8] or, "as he preferred to be called," Pachacuti, one of the kings of Tampu-tocco in the period of exile from Cuzco.[9] The first tradition of the Incas was that their ancestors, the earlier conquerors and "civilizers" of Peru, were descended from gods who appeared as white men and came to Cuzco from Lake Titicaca.

As the railway train from Lake Titicaca to Cuzco goes north up the pampa it passes, some thirty-seven miles

---

[6] *La Crónica del Perú* (Madrid), pp. 314-315.

[7] Cieza de Leon (Markham's translation), *Chronicle of Peru*, Hak. Soc., p. 4.

[8] Hiram Bingham, *Inca Land*, p. 308.

[9] Montesinos. Listed as the VIIth of this name. *Pachacuti* was a title of distinction meaning "Great Reformer." C. R. Markham, *The Incas of Peru*, p. 43.

The name Curi (Cari) appears in that of the Ayar Amauta Tupacuri, who was succeeded by his son of the same name in the dynasty of the Amautas preceding the kings of Tampu-tocco and the Incas. Montesinos (Hak. Soc.), pp. 54-55.

"In the time of this King (Tupac Curi Amauta) there came many

from the lake, a place among low spurs which are flung
into the plain from the converging mountains, where there
are "ruined buildings, mere heaps of stone, with human
figures carved upon them and other things worthy of
note." [10] These ruins mark the site of a frontier fortress
and outpost of the Ayar people on what was once the
boundary between their domain and that of the Collas,
who inhabited the Lake Titicaca region. Driven from
Tiahuanaco by the fierce nomad bowmen who swept up
from the south,—in the same manner as the Huns and
Tatars overran eastern Europe,—the Ayar leaders made
their stand here as they retreated north towards the valley
of the Vilcanota. To this day the place is called Pucará
(the fortress); it was the southernmost one of the line
of forts, many of them of megalithic construction, which
mark the successive stands of the great megalithic race of
builders as they struggled to retain the dominion of the
vast region of Lake Titicaca and the valleys of the Vilcanota and its tributaries.

In these struggles the Ayars left at various strategic
points in the line of their long retreat, covering the vast
area of their mountain pastures and terraced gardens, the

hordes of people from Tucumán, and his Governors retired towards
Cuzco. He assembled his forces and prepared a great army. He sent
spies to find out what manner of men the enemy were. He learned that
they were coming in two armies. He halted with his warriors on a high
pass full of snow, which is twenty leagues south of Cuzco, and which
is called Huillcanota. There fortified he awaited the enemy. He gave
battle to the first army, which he conquered easily on account of it being
in disorder. The second army, hearing the news, came very confusedly
to aid their fellows, and it also was conquered. The King entered
Cuzco triumphant, bearing before him the vanquished, naked and with their
hands tied. From this event the ancients called this king Huillcanota."
Montesinos (Hak. Soc.), pp. 55-6.

[10] Cieza de Leon, *Crónica*, etc., p. 320.

most stupendous works of masonry in the world. So many are the ruins of fortresses about this first line of defense at Pucará that a considerable region there came to be called Pucará. "The situation of the defensive works which we have pointed out; their location in strategic points, which defend against the arrival of attackers from the south; the magnitude of the fortifications which, starting from the impregnable fort of Pucará, proceed, multiplying themselves and extending their parapets and curtains, until they are fully developed in the Paucartambo-Limactambo zone just at the termination of the temperate valley of the Vilcanota and the interior gate of the paradisiacal valley of the Urubamba (a region 'very much harassed on account of being excessively beautiful'); the powerful and colossal fortification of Ollantaytambo in the very throat of the warm valley (a fortification which appears to exceed human power and which was erected by a people who made in it not only a defense but also a secure and luxurious refuge)—all these constructions and the many more which are further on, reveal in full and convincing proof, of monumental origin, not only the antiquity but the purpose and object of their construction." [11]

Ayaviri, fifty-seven miles from the lake, was the scene of desperate battles in successive wars, in some of which the slaughter was so great that "few or none remained alive." [12] "In ancient times this city of Ayaviri is said to have been a wonderful sight and it still is [in 1550 when Cieza de Leon visited it], especially the great sepulchers

[11] Horacio H. Urteaga, *Las Antiguas Civilizaciones y Razas del Perú* (Lima, 1921), p. 262.
[12] Cieza de Leon, *Crónica*, etc., p. 310.

it contains,—so many that they occupy more space than the dwellings of the living population." [13] As it was on the main thoroughfare of the Indians, taxes were collected here in kind, and there were "many depositories built into a small rock ridge where the tribute was stored." [14]

Ayavirí was "an important and principal place" and contained a temple of the sun, many "great palaces" and large inns. A "very good river" ran through the town and emptied into Lake Titicaca. It had its source twenty-two miles to the north in the knot of the Vilcanota, where it shared with the Amazon the waters of the dark tarn of La Raya. This river, like the region about it, was called Pucará, or Fort River, from the forts which guarded this "dark and bloody ground." The ancient city was protected in front by the fortress of Pucará and behind by the walls and forts of the pass and those in the upper valley of the Vilcanota.

To the north, towards the gap, the hills crowded further and further into the narrowing plain. It is a vast treeless grassland. The river runs at the foot of the hills on one side, then winds its way across the valley and follows the base of the opposite ridge. Lights and shadows play in the *quebradas*,—or "breaks" in the line of

[13] Cieza de Leon, *Crónica*, etc., pp. 309-10.

[14] *Id.*, p. 310. Other definitions are given of the word Ayavirí, but it is not unlikely that it is from Ayar (the king's title) and *viri* or *virá* (general storehouse). As to the meaning of *virá*, see Markham, *Incas*, etc., pp. 41, 42.

The variety of forms in which the Spanish chroniclers wrote down the spoken Quichua words as they heard them, and especially the word Ayar,— interchanging the position of the letters, abbreviating, etc.,—is shown in the name of the Ayar Amauta King, Tacco Capac, which appears in different places in Montesinos' *Memorias* as Ayar Taco, Ayatarco Cupc, Arartarco, and Arartarcotitu. Montesinos (Hak. Soc.), p. 39, note by T. A. Joyce.

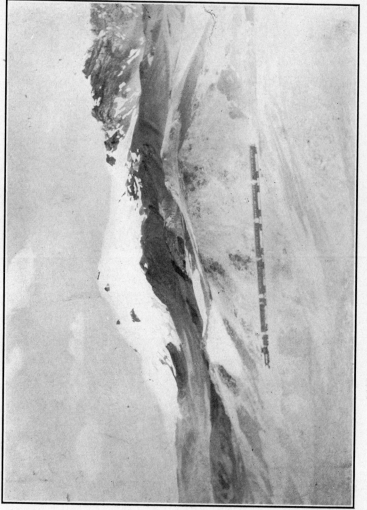

MOUNT VILCANOTA AND THE PASS OF LA RAYA

hills,—cañons and coulees which open on to the plain. As one passes, brown-backed quail,—their yellow breasts reflecting a glow of color as they rise from the grass at the roadside,—make short flights and settle down again on the prairie.

Here through the center of the valley, there mounting a little way along the base of the protruding hills, crossing at times the little river at some convenient ford when the stream lies athwart its course, runs the prehistoric road. Following the grade of the valley it climbs steadily to the pass. Ninety-nine miles from the lake it reaches the col in the "knot" of the Vilcanota, at an elevation of 14,153 feet above the sea. It skirts the dark pond of La Raya, lying on the "lap" of the very dividing ridge of the Andes, and passes down by the hot springs, four miles further on, to the "sacred valley" of the Vilcanota and the magic land of the Incas.

Familiarly close, as one passes the col, lie snow-fields on either hand, as though in one's yard. It is a cold and desolate landscape. The soil seems barren, but tame alpacas and llamas are grazing along the very edge of the snow-line where the grass is kept green by the many rills from the melting snow. In the bitter cold of the freezing nights the thawing ceases and the rivulets are dead; in the heat of the brilliant mountain sun they spring into life again.

The snow-fields on the east rise into glaciers on a rocky height 17,994 feet above the sea. This is Mount Vilcanota, the sentinel peak overlooking the ancient highway where it passes through the gap. This pass between the basin of Lake Titicaca and the valley of Cuzco and the

Vilcanota, north, is the key to the great thoroughfare along the axis of the Andes, over which moved the prehistoric migrations.

Though a rocky mountain road, it is still the main thoroughfare of the country. A barefooted Quichua peon in short jacket, loose knee-trousers and flat broad-brimmed hat,—a Chinese coolie in appearance,—passes by as night comes on, driving his pack-train of llamas, to stop at some desolate stone hut among the rocks. The strange Andean camels move with an aristocratic deliberation,— their ostrich-like heads, high in the air, and straight slender legs giving an impression of grace and fastidiousness as they daintily pick their way, their short tails jauntily curled. The ancestors of both peon and llamas have passed and repassed on this spot for more than 4,000 years.

The road is merely a broad trail beaten into the clay and gravel of the earth by the feet of men and llamas. There is a network of pathways. Over these have passed tribes in flight, armies on the march, kings in triumphal procession, captives in bonds, and the heralds of new cultures before Rome was built. When Europe was a wilderness, its forests and seaports inhabited by rude savages, a cultured race carried on its communications and waged its wars over this highway.

In prehistoric times a wall extended from the snow-line on one side to that on the other, with a gate through which travelers passed. "With the fall of Ayavirí, the invasion of the Collas extended without difficulty through the plateau to the boundary at La Raya. The two hostile races had this boundary line between their dominions.

Very near La Raya, this '*divortia aquarum*' of the basins of the Vilcanota and of the river Chuncará or Ayavirí [now called the Pucará],—natural barrier ridge which separates the temperate lands from the cold pampas of Titicaca,—ran a long wall of defense against invasion.

"Already tumbled down in the epoch of the Incas, its origin and construction became the subject of legends. It was supposed that this defensive work marked the boundary between dominions of the Collas and the Quichuas in a very recent epoch,—although the antiquity of the buildings, their architectural style, and the fact that the Inca annalists were entirely silent as to its construction by the Incas, contradict the legend. Today there are no traces left of this work of most extreme antiquity; but we can reconstruct it, guided by the description of Father Lizárraga, who visited it between 1590 and 1600. 'Returning to our lake of Vilcanota,' he says, 'a little further on, about half a league, we see a stone wall of rubble which runs from the snow on one side of the pass to the snow on the other, across the royal highway. This wall, the aged people say, was made by agreement between the Incas and the Indians of Collao, who, having carried on various fierce wars between themselves, came together on this middle ground to construct this boundary wall in this place about the height of a man and not very thick; which should serve as a rampart so that the Incas should not pass it to conquer Collao nor the Collas to Cuzco. This boundary wall can be seen today, from the snow of one hill crossing a valley and the royal highway and rising to the snow on the other hill.' " [15]

[15] Urteaga, *supra*, pp. 253-4.

This was the battle-gap of the Ayars,—the Ther-
mopylæ (well so called, as here, also, were hot springs,
at *Aguas Calientes*) of the Andes.

In this gap, for untold centuries, men struggled for the
dominion of the matchless valley of the Vilcanota. The
religion of Viracocha, the culture of the Amautas, the caste
of the Ayar nobles, the empire of the Incas, all depended
on the issue of battles fought in this pass. The golden
glory of sunset on the snow fields of these sentinel hills
has darkened into night and left unsettled the issue while
men fought here for land and empire. The fate of races
and of a continent hung upon the issue of the combat. As
the leaf on the waters of the tarn around which they
struggled is borne by a gust of wind to the right or left
and may float to the far Atlantic or find an outlet on the
Pacific side into the distant marshes of Poopo,—so, not
once but many times, on this high pass of the prehistoric
road forces that might have ripened into a far more brilliant culture and changed the destiny of a continent hung
upon the balance of fate in a fitful struggle.

Through this battle-gap passed the first Ayars on their
migration from Titicaca to Cuzco. The megalithic builders of Sacsahuaman passed over the same road. Here
the white race of man-gods [16] made their stand against the

[16] The universal tradition of the Peruvians of gods in the form of white
men was common to all branches of the Aryan race and to the darker
peoples with whom they came in contact, and no doubt was based, on the
one hand, on the arrogant pride of the superiority of the white man, and,
on the other, on the recognition of this superiority by the darker races.
Among our own people the conception of angels as very blond, in the
human form, is but a parcel of the same racial belief. The title of
Viracocha, given by the mountain Quichuas of Peru to the white Spanish
conquerors, and the exclamation of the Romans, *"Angeli!"* on sight of
the white-skinned, yellow-headed Teutons, are parallel illustrations of
this racial idea.

darker indigenous hordes from the south and in other times against new incursions, probably migrations of branches of their own dominant race from the Western Islands. In this pass of the condensed and knotted Andes, Tituyupanqui, Pachacuti VI,—sixty-fourth king of the long line of the dynasties of the Piruas and the Amautas who preceded the Incas,—carried on his royal litter at the head of his Quichua soldiers in desperate battle, was killed by an arrow.[17]

When Pachacuti fell the Amauta dynasty came to an end. The rude hordes from the south swarmed through the gap of La Raya into the beautiful valley of Vilcanota

[17] Bingham, *Inca Land*, p. 120, citing Montesinos.

As a local and secondary line of defense, north of the pass, in the upper Vilcanota valley at Urcos, there was "a great wall with a wide gate where were stationed gatekeepers who collected taxes and levies imposed by the lords of the country. There were also stationed at this portal of the lower Vilcanota officers of the Incas whose business it was to arrest and punish any who dared to carry gold and silver away from the city of Cuzco." (Cieza de Leon, *Crónica*, etc., Madrid, p. 307.)

The wall of Urcos, like that at Ollantaytambo, was an aqueduct and carried a stream of water across the valley.

Montesinos tells of "marvels and portents which appeared in the sky each day with a great variety of comets and a continuous trembling of the earth and destruction of buildings," and of a "multitude of tribes which came from all directions, publishing the tidings of the destruction and expulsion of the inhabitants of the kingdom." There were prognostications of misfortune by soothsayers.

"News was received that many hordes of warriors were marching through the Collao and that their ferocious men, who were going through the Andes, were approaching and that they had some black men among them; and the same was said of the coasts. . . . Titu Upanqui, with the main body of his army, arrived at the high mountains which bear the name of Pucará and he built many Andenes, trenches, and so on in such a way that they each had but one very narrow entrance leading to the first platform of the mountain and having another athwart it, and so on, all the way up to the very highest of all where the King had his stores and the necessary supplies. . . . Being thus fortified, the King set forth to give battle, which was a very fierce one. Titu Upanqui received a stroke from an arrow while he was going about in all directions, encouraging his men from his golden litter." Montesinos (Hak. Soc.), pp. 59-61.

and overran the seats of culture. The followers of Pachacuti retreated with his body into the fastnesses of the
Vilcapampa,—the lovely mountain region of varied pasture and forest, situated among the snow peaks between
the Urubamba and the Apurimac.[18]

In this retreat, in this or some such exile in the long
history of the race, they built the marvelous city of Machu
Picchu on its beetling granite ridge, and the impregnable
fort of Salapunco of megalithic ashlar masonry at the
narrows of the Urubamba River below Ollantaytambo,—
for the protection of the delectable valley below, with its
terraced gardens.

At times, in the hand-to-hand fighting in the battle-gap,
the slaughter was so great that the dead could not be
buried and tradition relates that plagues were started
from the reeking bodies which covered the ground.[19]

A long period of barbarism,—the "Dark Ages" of the
Ayar tradition,—followed the fall of the Amautas. The
country was divided into warring tribes and given over to
unnatural sins and the worship of strange idols. Many
centuries later the descendants of the Ayars under Ayar
Manco emerged with their followers from Tampu-tocco
(Vilcapampa) and reestablished the worship of Viracocha
and the dominion of their race in Cuzco.

They gradually extended their rule again to the gap of
La Raya, which was again a battle-field, and carried their

---

[18] Bingham, *Inca Land,* pp. 306-7.
[19] "Titu Upanqui's men secretly carried off his body and deposited it in
Tamputocco; later they sent Ambassadors to ask leave to inter the dead,
to the enemy, who were celebrating their victory with great banquets.
Leave was not granted and in a short while the air was befouled and
defiled so that almost the whole of both armies was exterminated." . . .
Montesinos (Hak. Soc.), pp. 61-2.

dominion further on to Ayavirí and Pucará. In later generations the armies of the great Pachacuti Inca Upanqui and his son Tupac Inca Upanqui carried the rainbow standard of the Ayars beyond the fortresses which guarded the gap of Vilcanota, and added Chile and Tucumán to their empire.[20]

[20] They never, however, conquered the Araucanian Indians of southern Chile; nor did the Spaniards.

II

TIAHUANACO

And, as the stars wink out upon the blue,
The Titans turn their questioning eyes to heaven;
The starry answer is a question too:
"Ah! whither are we driven?"

J. MACMILLAN BROWN, *The Riddle of the Pacific*.

ON the Bolivian "alto-plane," 12,520 feet above the sea, in what was formerly Upper Peru, and not far from the present international boundary, stand the monumental ruins of prehistoric Peru which bear the most unmistakable resemblance to those of Mexico and Central America. Low hills rise on either side towards the sierras to the east and west. In the very trough of the ancient lake,—now the inter-cordilleran plateau,—some twelve miles from the port of Guaqui, on the present southern extremity of the great Andean Lake Titicaca, the stone carvings of *Tiahuanaco* record the same primitive culture as that of Chavin in northern Peru and the aboriginal art of *Teotihuacan* on the high plateau of Mexico.

The terraced pyramid of Tiahuanaco surmounted by the sacred structures of the high-place is but a continuation of the type of early Toltec structures about Lake *Texcoco* (Peruvian counterpart, *Titicaca*). The great quadrangular enclosure around the ruins of a palace of cut stone, near this pyramid, displays very much the same arrangement in this holy place on the high table-land of Bolivia,

40

TIAHUANACO

ENTRANCE TO GREAT QUADRANGLE, TIAHUANACO

Note how the steps are worn by centuries of use, and by the weather.

inhabited from prehistoric times by an Aymará race, as the Mayan ruins of Copán and Oaxaca. The symbolic low-relief carvings on the monolithic gateway at Tiahuanaco, like those on the stone of Chavin, indicate the same method and considerable of the conventional detail employed upon tablets, pottery, and pictures of prehistoric Mexico.

Monoliths of red sandstone, some of them ten feet in height, dressed and squared, enclose in perfect alignment a rectangular space extending lengthwise ten degrees from east and west 388 by 445 feet in size. Within the enclosure, though its ruins have been preyed upon for centuries for building-stone for the church and other buildings in the neighboring village, are still left the foundations of extensive structures of exquisite and admirable masonry.[1]

A great stone idol, crudely carved, clutching the conventional scepters of power, stands near the southwest corner. A broad megalithic stairway of seven steps leads between two square piers of dressed stone, in the eastern line of the enclosure, to the raised plane within. At the opposite end near the northwest corner is a remarkable gateway carved and polished from a single block of hard trachyte brought from a distant quarry. It is elaborately ornamented in low relief with the figures of a god and of forty-eight other gods or rulers making obeisance to him.

The principal figure occupies a position immediately over the entrance. He holds in either hand his staff

[1] Squier, *Land of the Incas*, p. 279.

of authority. As with the Chavin god,[2] serpents and conventional rays stream from his headdress and belt. The puma also appears. Condors' heads form the feet of the throne upon which he stands. The scepters which he holds, though they seem to be writhing like snakes, end in the heads of birds, and that in his left hand is divided at the top, each extremity terminating in the head of a condor, while a crested condor-head also forms its base.

To the right and left of this central figure extend three panels of smaller figures, eight in each panel on each side,—forty-eight in all. Each tributary figure holds a scepter and makes obeisance, kneeling on one knee, to the central figure. They have the human form except that they all have wings and those in the central panel on each side have the heads of falcons or eagles. They wear crowns of serpents' and condors' heads and their tunics and bodies are likewise adorned with the same emblems. A curious detail is that the scepters of the figures in the two upper panels end in serpents' heads while those of the figures in the lower panel are like the scepters of the central figure and terminate in the heads of condors. An elaborately carved frieze runs underneath these panels, in which the same *motif* predominates,—human faces encircled in rays and serpents, buglers, conventional lines and angles skillfully carved, ornamented with the heads of condors and serpents.

Just outside of the southeastern corner of the enclosure stood a great terraced rectangular pyramid now largely in ruins from the excavations of treasure-hunters.

[2] *Infra*, Vol. I, p. 139; Vol. II, p. 47.

MONOLITHIC GATE AT TIAHUANACO

The falcon-headed gods and divine Kings worshipping the Creator. The repetition of the figures emphasizes the devotion, and represents repeated obeisances, like a moving picture. The rod by the side, sunk to the base, which was buried, indicates the height of the stone to be 3 meters.

DETAIL OF MONOLITHIC GATE, TIAHUANACO

This is the left extremity of the lower border of the frieze. Professor Arthur Posnansky quite plausibly suggests that the faces represent the sun in the several months,—the bugler, with his bugle turned towards the center of the calendar, indicating the turn of the sun at the solstice back towards the equator.

From Markham's "Incas of Peru."

It is 620 feet long, 450 feet wide, 50 feet high, and its sides lie parallel with those of the megalithic enclosure. The terraces of the pyramid were sustained by walls of handsomely cut and fitted stones, ornamented with carvings of elaborate design. Sacrificial buildings stood upon the summit of the high-place.

Long before the ancestor of the Incas was reported to have been born of the Sun out of the water of Lake Titicaca and founded, with his sister-wife, the race of conquerors whose myths relate that they went from the Island of the Sun, by long wanderings, to found the city of Cuzco towards the north, the despots of Tiahuanaco commandeered the labor of an enslaved people and set over them their master masons. By what wave of tribal conquest they themselves were overthrown remains yet to be deciphered from the unwritten history of the successive invasions which, in the course of ages, have swept over the high valleys of the Andes.[3]

[3] Specifically discussing the remains of archaic ceramic art in Central and South America in an interesting article published in the *Boletín de la Sociedad Geográfica de Lima*, XXXIII (1917), Philip Ainsworth Means, M.A., says:

"It appears to me that the Chimus, the Yuncas, and the other coastal nations of Peru were in great part derived from the people of the archaic culture. But we must record that the emigrations from Central America to South America continued to take place in later periods. To remember this clarifies the fact that in the primitive civilizations in the northern part of the Peruvian littoral there are contained many elements obviously derived from the culture of Central America. Such were the enormous pyramids of the temples. Such also were the elegant decorations of pottery.

". . . In short we can say that the comparison of the date of the archaic type in Central America reveals that by the beginning of the Christian era, more or less, this archaic culture and its creators began to arrive on the coast of Peru, and that an evolution similar to that of Central America started in Peru, stimulated from time to time by new casual immigration from the north. The superficial likeness between the art of Peru and the art of Central America is explained by the common psychology of the two parts of the race, fundamentally only one. In the same way are explained the analogies between the cultures of eastern Siberia and those of Alaska and the west coast of Canada."

The archaic migrations from Central America to Peru, both along the coast and in the high plateau, such as those from which were developed the civilizations of Bogotá and Quito, probably began many centuries before the date suggested by Mr. Means.

The extract quoted is a curious example of what might be called the obsession of the doctrine of local, independent, autochthonous development of similar cultures in different localities. After stating that "many elements" of the Peruvian "primitive civilizations" "are obviously derived from the culture of Central America," and that the Peruvians themselves were "in great part derived" from Central America, this distinguished writer cannot resist injecting the contradictory stock remark that the similarity of the two cultures is "explained by the common psychology." He does not tell us what the implied abandonment by the immigrants of all their native racial arts is "explained by."

Moses B. Cotsworth ("The Pre-Inca Calendar," *West Coast Leader*, Vol. 18, No. 940, Lima, February 18, 1930, p. 26) discusses an article by Professor Arthur Posnansky "published in *Das Weltall*, Jahrgang 24; Heft 2, by Dr. F. S. Archenbold, Director of the Treptow Observatory in Berlin." The theory is set out in detail that the sculptures on the monolithic gate at Tiahuanaco are a sun calendar, marking the solstices, equinoxes, and the twelve months of six five-day weeks each,—as contrasted with the Mexican calendar of eighteen months, each of four five-day weeks.

The method of observation of the setting sun by sighting through the opening of the gate over sun columns to the west, as set out in this article, is not clear in its relation to the actual situation of the monolithic gate and the frieze upon it which faces nearly east; but there can be no doubt that the great alignment at Tiahuanaco, like the Inti-huatanas in other Peruvian temples, had its part in the solar observations and records by which the daily occupations and religious life of the people were governed.

It may well be that the figures in the frieze represent the Creator in the center, the Sun in the twelve divisions of the Zodiac, and the division of time into months, weeks, and days.

III

THE SACRED VALLEY

THE enormous watershed which collects the drainage from the stupendous masses of snow and ice on the eastern slopes of the mighty rampart of the *Cordillera Real,* and its extensions to the north and south, feeds through its great fan-shaped system of innumerable watercourses the Madre de Dios, the Beni, and the Mamoré. Like great arteries of the earth, these mighty rivers collect, through a network of veins in the cañons of the mountain slopes and the forested plains at their eastern base, the tremendous rainfall of the highlands and converge in equal angles to form the Madeira,—greatest tributary and rival of the Amazon.

Breaking off opposite the northern part of Lake Titicaca, the mighty range, after a partial recession, is renewed in the snowy sierras forming the ganglion, or "knot," of the Vilcanota. Through the heart of these titanic masses of granite the Vilcanota river has cut its way in a stupendous serpentine gorge. Under the successive names of Vilcamayu, Yucay, Vilcanota, and Urubamba, it flows from the pastures of alpacas among the snows about La Raya through long and secluded glens of perpetual spring into flowering forests of endless but salubrious summer to form, at its junction with the Apurimac, the super-river Ucayali,—carrying its yellow flood far to the north to

45

join the Amazon more than one thousand miles above the mouth of the Madeira.

The secluded sunny vale of the Vilcanota was the "Sacred Valley" of the Incas. In the lovely glen of Yucay and on the towering peak of Pisac, along the pleasant streams that flow into the sacred river at Ollantay-tambo, on the granite ridge of Machu Picchu, along the temperate zone of the valley, below the cold of the plateau and above the heat of the lowlands, amid panoramas of snowy peaks but bathed in the warmth and sunshine of spring, the kindred but perpetually warring tribes who preceded the conquests of the Incas constructed their superb temples, their high-places, their sacrificial altars of the sun, their hanging gardens, terraced mountains, matchless aqueducts, paved roads, massive fortresses, impressive tombs, and the villas and palaces of their kings.

The imperial Inca road to Chinchay-Suyu, the northern quarter of the kingdom, climbed the hill back of Cuzco to the edge of the plain of Anta overlooking the city. A narrow-gauge railway now follows this route. The Incarial highway, after crossing this famous plain, the battle-field of warring tribes from immemorial times, descended to the west into the great cañon of the Apuri-mac and after crossing this gorge passed on to the north towards Quito.

The modern mule track follows the same route, by Abancay and Ayacucho. Quite recently an automobile road has been opened between Ayacucho and Huancayo and from Huancayo a railroad follows the high plateau track of prehistoric migrations as far north as Gollaris-

CURVED TERRACES AND FORMAL GARDENS IN
FRONT OF RUINS OF AN INCA PALACE, VALLEY
OF THE VILCANOTA

Note also the stone diking by which the river is confined
in a straight course, and the remarkable series of stone-walled
terraces on the steep side of the mountain.

*Photograph taken by the author from the height
on which the temple of Pisac is situated.*

guisgua,—with a branch tunneling the crest of the western cordillera and passing thence down the cañon of the Rimac to the Pacific at Callao.[1]

On the east the plain of Anta [2] breaks upon the steeps that lead down to the valley of the Vilcamayu, overlooking its lovely gardens,—with a view of the snow ranges of the Paucartambo and Tres Cruces on the horizon.

Near where the little railroad passes through the stony eastern barrier of the plain into the picturesque gorge of the Chospiyoc are the terraced gardens of a prehistoric Indian noble. Rising tier on tier upon the base of the bordering hills splendid walls of faced stone, following in graceful and parallel curves the bend of the land, support a series of enriched and leveled terraces, watered by a never-failing rill from the hills behind, carried in nicely constructed channels down the succession of gardens.

The ancient highroad to the north, over which marched and fought the armies of Pachacuti, Tupac, and Huayna Ccapac,—the founders and consolidators of the greater Inca empire,—passes before this princely seat. Here met the armies of Huascar and Atahualpa, the rival brothers, and settled the heirship of the empire. Here appeared the fearful apparition of white men mounted on beasts shod with iron, who had fallen upon the Inca still absorbed in the heat of this domestic conflict in which blood was still flowing. The old migrations of ancestral tribes, long since forgotten even to tradition, passed over this old

[1] From the railroad point of view the road to Callao is the main line.

[2] In strict conformity with the geographical idiosyncrasies of the country, this famous plain has many names,—among them Suriti, Xaquixaguana, and Ychupampa.

road and left, as one of their enduring traces, this magnificent seat of rural elegance.

The little Chospiyoc gathers its waters on the famous
plain, partially drains the swamps which cover a portion
of the flats, and makes its noisy descent through its
picturesque cañon to the Vilcanota. Above on the plain
the storms break in magnificent fury, cold winds sweep
across the open plateau and chill one to the bone. Hardy
waterfowl,—white-breasted, black-winged, rather small
wild geese, ducks, ibises, cormorants, white and grey
gulls, plover, and snipe, are still more or less plentiful in
the marshy lands.

Passing down the rocky gorge of the Chospiyoc by its
"talking stream," one soon comes in the Sacred Valley
to a very different scene. It is protected from the wind
by the serried ramparts of hills which flank its tortuous
course. The nights are cool and refreshing; the almost
perpetual sunshine of the days is not oppressive. Showers
brighten the foliage and freshen the face of nature. The
rains are supplemented by systems of irrigation,—great
aqueducts across the face of the mountain, bringing to
elaborate terraced gardens the waters of vigorous streams
from far back in distant cañons.

In the upper Vilcanota, at an altitude of seven to eleven
thousand feet, and along this same belt throughout the
Peruvian Sierras, robins are plentiful, larger than our
"redbreasts," and of a slaty color, but identical in form,
habits, motions, and song. Higher up towards the central
plateau, flickers,[3] the mountain blue-bird, small red-tailed
hawks, a black-and-white carrion hawk, owls, and several

---

[3] In some places in the States called "yellow-hammers."

varieties of hardy sparrows find abundant food and, where there are no trees, nest among the rocks. A scrubby juniper grows in scattered patches in some of the higher cañons, but for wide stretches even this fails, and birds, whose kindred species in the north-temperate zone build their nests either in holes in trees or among the branches, change their habits to suit their surroundings and nest on the ground in the treeless plateau of the Andes.

The great charm of Peru is the varied assortment of climates so easily available. From the invigorating but harsh winds, the snow and sleet of the pampas, it is but an easy ride to the perennial spring of the middle valleys; and the fruits and flowers of the teeming tropics are but a few hours further on.

The cañon of the Chospiyoc debouches into the Vilcamayu a little above Ollantaytambo. In May the cornfields are heavy with the ripening crop. A mellow autumn sun, softened by a filmy haze, cures the great shocks of corn and hardens the piles of shucked grain spread out upon drying-beds in the edge of the ancient village.

Long lines of men,—clothed in their typical short trousers, Chinese pan-shaped hats, and wearing their inevitable ponchos over their shoulders even while they work,—with great loads of freshly cut corn upon their backs, pass in single file from the fields to the shucking grounds at the hacienda house, or on the borders of the village. So they and their ancestors have worked for ten thousand years. Neither beasts of burden nor modern farm machines have supplanted the primitive cheapness

of hand labor.   Women and children shuck and spread
the corn to dry as it is brought in.   The land seems to glow
in the restful maturity of the completed year, like the
Indian-summer of the Appalachians.

Far up the same Sacred Valley in the higher altitudes
around Sicuani the scene is quite different,—though it is
also harvest time there.   Oxen are treading out the wheat
spread in the open upon the "threshing floors,"—circular plots, some enclosed with a rim of rocks, some mere
level patches of ground tramped hard by use, over which
mules or horses or oxen are driven at a run until the grain
is tramped out from the head.   The straw is then removed
and, when there is a breeze, the grain is stirred about and
thrown into the air until the chaff is blown away.   Still
higher up the valley quinoa, an ancient Indian grain belonging to the spinach family, and haba, a rank-growing
large flat black bean, are also gathered in small shocks,
and, when dry, are beaten out with flails, and cleaned in
a similar manner by the wind.

The great harvest festivals, adopted by the sagacious
church from the pagan customs, will soon be held as the
crops are gathered.   As we rode in the early morning
from the modern village of Pisac in its entrancing vale
of Yucay at the foot of its terraced mountain on which
stands the marvelous temple and high altar of their ancestors, we passed,—along the brawling Taray which in
its deep quebrada flows here into the Vilcanota,—eager
parties of Quichuas, principally young women, dressed
in their picturesque costumes, hastening down the trail
with their strange swinging trot, past the historic ruins
of ancient villages, hurrying eagerly to the first of the

harvest *fiestas* in the hamlet below,—festivals and orgies as old as the ruins. Many of the travelers came from the little pueblos and chacras in the cañon,—small settlements sheltered by the hills and watered by quiet streams taken above from the same brook, which foams so boisterously past in the glen below. The water is brought in long ditches to the gardens and little farms.

Some of the barefooted Indian women who hurried by in their flaring, bright-colored multiple skirts, swinging their arms in front of them as they trotted along, with babies or bundles of food, clothing, and a few spoons and small cooking utensils, tied up in packs carried high on their backs, came from the pasture lands where they had left their sheep or llamas on the high grass ridges and pampas above.

Expectant and interested in the mysteries and rites of which the church would tell them, but still more perhaps in the music, the dance, the *chicha*, the *pisco* [4] and the night-long revels of the ancient harvest festival, they hastened to their rendezvous in the Sacred Valley. So they gathered from the pastured hills and from all the lovely valleys and glens pouring their waters into the Vilcanota about their ancient sacrificial peak of Pisac.

Though it was autumn many flowers still bloomed about Ollantaytambo and great brown and green humming-birds, as large as waxwings, were gathering the captive insects from the flower cups.

The valley is very narrow, the high mountains on both sides crowding close to the swift-flowing stream. At

---

[4] *Chicha*—a home-made beer, made from maize; *pisco*—a native grape brandy from the coast.

Ollantaytambo it is scarcely a mile from base to base of the hills,—widening to two or more lower down. In some places the valley contracts so that there is scarcely room for the passage of the rushing waters. The upper valley about Sicuani is wider. Since the coming of the Spaniards, at least, perhaps for a much longer time, nothing has been done to renew the marvelous soil of the terraces. It has produced crops of maize for centuries. It is not strange that at present, while the growing corn seems luxuriant, the yield of grain is small,—twenty bushels per acre being considered a large crop.

The wonder is that it produces anything at all. For hundreds of years nothing has been done to repair the ditches or marvelous terrace walls, here and there falling into decay, allowing the water to wash out the fields and road. But so perfect was the work of the ancient builders who in the dim past preceded not only the Spaniards but the Inca conquerors,—conquerors who like the Spaniards enjoyed the fruits of those whom they conquered and enslaved,—that the agriculture of the valley is still maintained by the same system of irrigation, the same aqueducts, the same leveled and terraced fields as when they were first constructed in the prehistoric past.

From many points in the winding narrow valley can be seen, rising above the mountain walls which enclose the cultivated area, the sharp snow peak of Chicón,[5] wrapped in its fog or shrouded in thick snow-storms. In the high zone of the mountain range, on the slopes watered by the melting glaciers and snow-fields, the grass grows green and makes a lovely contrast of color. In the deep and

[5] Also called Veronica.

sunny valley there is little rain, and the support of the dense population which made possible the stupendous works in which it abounds depended upon ingenious systems of irrigation.

IV

THE TEMPLES OF THE SUN AND THE MOON

In the lower part of Cuzco, below the palaces, but with a clear view down the valley of the Cachimayo towards the rising sun, stood the adjoining temples of the sun and moon. The walls enclosed a considerable block of land on a "bench," with a little stream, formed by the three brooklets, gurgling at its base in the rear. The great entrance portal opened into a handsome hall, and from this, through doorways and corridors of classic taste and simplicity, access was had to a succession of rooms, holy places of the stars and lesser deities. There were quarters also within the temple for the priests.

The long walls of the "house of the sacred virgins" stand near by, and no doubt there was a secret underground entrance,—a part of the system of passage-tunnels of which many have been discovered but none thoroughly explored. The halls, corridors, and rooms of the temples, really a joint-temple of the sun and moon, were separated by an inner wall of matchless workmanship from a great court filled with idols of gold and silver, in imitation of animals and plants held sacred in the animistic phases of the religion of the Quichuas.

Even among the marvelously constructed edifices of Cuzco, the temples of the sun and moon were distinguished by the perfection of the work bestowed upon

54

them. Every stone was cut with exact accuracy into a suitable polyhedron, smoothed upon all sides, laid without mortar in regular rows, joined to each other with such nicety, layer interlocked with layer with such consummate art that with few exceptions the frequent earthquakes of centuries have not dislodged them in any perceptible degree.

The northwestern part of the combined temples was enclosed in a curved instead of a straight wall. Inclining towards the interior in a perfectly graded angle from foundation to capping and at the same time curving in exterior convex lines with mathematical precision and regularity, each stone fitting with such perfection that the wall is as symmetrical as though it were cut from one solid rock, it demonstrates a skill, patience, perseverance, and supreme command of resources (labor) comparable with any masonry in the world.

Before it was despoiled to pay the ransom of Atahualpa, and its remaining treasures hidden by the priests or seized by its fanatical and greedy captors, the interior of the temple was gorgeously adorned in gold, silver, and precious stuffs. Brilliantly dyed fabrics of vicuña wool, of the finest texture, hung upon the walls and before the holy places. Luxurious rugs of elegant design and skillful workmanship covered the floors and were spread upon the stone benches built in here and there at the base of the walls. Idols of precious metals stood in the sacred recesses and a golden image of the sun streamed with the morning light which fell through an open doorway upon the western interior wall of the temple. A broad band of beaten gold extended around the exterior of the walls like a gorgeous frieze.[1]

The interior was corniced and studded with gold and even today small particles of this rich adornment which have escaped the avaricious hand of the spoiler may be seen adhering to the rock. Some of the severe but superb megalithic doorframes have been torn away from their solid setting, with much difficulty, by the Spanish priests to give place to rounded arches of poorly cut stone put crudely together with daubs of mortar.

The ancient temple of the Incas has been built over with the mongrel and tawdry structures of a decadent Gothic-Moorish type of monastery and church. Rubble and crumbling plaster, makeshift beams of rough wood with protruding ends, additions of cane and adobe have surmounted, as though burying in a pile of rubbish, the chaste and massive walls. The golden image of the sun and the polished and precious idols in their simple niches on the walls are gone and in their place a heterogeneous assortment of idols of wood and wax cluttered with cheap and gaudy gewgaws and the accumulated dust of years. Dominican priests occupy the quarters of the royal hierarchy of the sun.

[1] Prescott.

THE CURVED BUTTRESS OF ONE OF THE WALLS OF THE
PRE-INCA TEMPLE OF THE SUN AND MOON AT CUZCO

It shows a slight dislocation from an earthquake. It is now used as a
foundation of the Dominican Monastery, the Spanish Conquerors having
turned over to that Order the Ayar Sanctuary. Note the stones in the
Spanish masonry above taken from the incomparably finer walls which
the Spaniards destroyed. The finish of some of the interior walls is even
finer than this buttress.

Photograph by Mancilla, Arequipa.

Sacsahuaman and the plain (in the foreground) lying between it and the pedestals of the *huacos* on the Rodadero (which is not within view of the picture). The size of the fortress can be appreciated by noting the people seated on the front wall in the centre. Note the angles in the wall. On top of the hill in the background three towers stood in ancient times. They were torn down by the Spaniards to obtain building material for use in Cuzco, which lies over the hill to the rear. A glimpse of the Cuzco valley can be seen in the distance in the left of the picture.

V

SACSAHUAMAN

Who made their mates of stone to fall they know,
What tyrant broke their golden thread of fate;
They turn their backs upon their ruthless foe,
Their looks all scorn and hate.

J. MACMILLAN BROWN, *The Riddle of the Pacific.*

JOINING and overlooking Cuzco on its northern side lies the hill of Sacsahuaman. Many Inca remains are referred to as fortresses which were primarily of an entirely different character,—open temples. But Sacsahuaman was the great fortress of Cuzco. It is said that on the advent of the Spaniards three tall stone towers crowned the very summit of the hill and constituted the center of the defensive works. These towers have now entirely disappeared,—their stones used by the Spaniards for building in the city. Prescott, however, gives a dramatic picture of the storming and capture of one of them by Juan Pizarro, where, in his reckless bravery, he received the wound of which he died two weeks later. His brother Hernando attacked and took the other two,—a powerful Inca noble, who had stood upon the parapet on the summit of one beating off assailants with great strength and courage, finally casting himself headlong to his death rather than surrender.

Below these towers a strong wall ran around the steep hill on three sides, constituting, with the declivity of the hill itself, its outer defense and merging on the northeast side, furthest from the city, with the triple-terraced series of angled walls of megaliths, which, by reason of their enormous size as well as the skill with which they are laid together, remain today exactly as they were originally placed,—defying the energy or even the power of a conqueror to dislodge or transport them.

The huge stones of which this fortress is constructed are of soft blue limestone, easily worked, and were quarried from a ledge in the limestone hills a mile or more away to the north, and transported over very uneven ground to their present position. One of them is 27 feet in length, 14 feet in width, and 12 feet thick.[1] Many of them are but little smaller and are placed together in the Cyclopean fortress with as much accuracy and close-fitting, though irregular, alignment as the walls of smaller stones of the imperial temples and palaces of Cuzco.

Some feet back of the first wall and terrace is a second one of less height and somewhat smaller stones, but scarcely less remarkable. Behind this is a third parapet of similar construction but still smaller size, and behind this the hill rises steeply to the point where the inner towers formerly stood. All three walls are a constant succession of angles and recessions, on a method quite approved by military science until such forts became more or less obsolete as a result of the experience gained with high-explosive shells in the great World War.

The height of the first wall of the fort is 27 feet and the width of the terrace behind, between it and the second wall, is 35 feet. In a surprise attack at night the entire

[1] Measurements by Squier.

DETAIL OF THE MASONRY OF SACSAHUAMAN

Mrs. Poindexter on the horse. Captain E. M. S. Steward standing by
the great monolith in the wall of the fortress.

Photograph by the author.

series of ramparts and parapets could easily have been scaled by ladders. The entrance through the walls was by way of narrow portals, clumsily sealed in an emergency with great stones kept ready for that purpose. It is claimed [2] that Juan Pizarro found one of these gateways and succeeded in the darkness, in the midst of fierce resistance, in removing the stone which blocked it, and rode his horse into the citadel. Possession of the fort would not necessarily have prevented an enemy from entering and destroying or looting the city, so far as its massive structure permitted it to be destroyed or looted. So long as the "acropolis" was held, however, towering above the city, which lay within reach of firebrands and ancient missiles of war, the continued occupation of the city by an enemy would have been difficult if not impossible.

The great fortress faced to the north, on the side opposite from the city, immediately upon a perfectly level field of a few acres extending between it and the limestone dike of the *Rodadero* a little further to the north. An enemy attacking the fort in its front must necessarily pass across this level open field to the very base of the parapet, exposed at every step to the missiles of its defenders. On the other hand any person exposed to view within the fort was within range of archers partly protected behind the *Rodadero*. It is probable, notwithstanding the walls and steepness of the ground on the other sides, that the fort was more vulnerable from another approach than by the great megalithic ramparts. At any rate the tremendous works did not prevent a handful of determined Spaniards from taking and holding the city,

[2] Prescott.

though its grass roofs were burned around their station in the public square,—nor from storming and capturing the fortress itself.

The tremendous stronghold seems to Have been the product of pride and fear. It could only have been built by a monarch who commanded the unpaid labor of a multitude,—either his own subjects or a captive people. Combined with a boastful pride and vanity which speak from the size, durability, and perfection of the work, it tells also of terror. In its extraordinary and exaggerated but blind preparations for defense, it records a terrible fear which experience or tradition had instilled in a ruler, perhaps in a whole people, of attack by some dreaded, some fierce and powerful enemy. In the dread of overwhelming assault of which it so eloquently speaks, in the patience, skill, endurance, and cheapness of the labor required for its construction, in the autocratic authority which alone could command such labor, it is comparable with the Great Wall erected by the Chinese as a supreme effort to protect themselves from the horror of the northern barbarian hordes.

And one was as futile for its purpose as the other. Neither stayed the march of the conqueror. As an expression of power, a memorial of pride, it is comparable with the great pyramids of Egypt. Its construction required the labor of thousands for many years. It endures, and probably will endure as long as or longer than the pyramids, but the name of the monarch or succession of monarchs at whose word a people slaved has been completely forgotten.

Like most works of the Peruvian Ayars, the stupendous ramparts of Sacsahuaman indicate an art which was promising but which never reached its full expression. They were undoubtedly constructed at a very early epoch, perhaps begun as the very first work of a people who had been driven into this remote location and resolved as their first act to make themselves secure, perhaps with the enslaved labor of the indigenous people whom they, in turn, had overrun,—as the Aztec-Toltec invasion developed the architectural glories of the decadent Maya city of Chichen-Itza, by the slave labor of its former rulers.

In the huge size of the stones employed, combined with the knowledge of the art of military fortification displayed, Sacsahuaman is distinct. But in many respects it gives unmistakable proof of the contact and kinship of the culture of its builders with those of Cuzco, Pisac, and Machu Picchu, different though in many respects the conception of each is from the others. In the irregular angles of the stones fitted in perfect union without mortar, in the peculiar method of locking stone into stone, it is identical with some of the structures of Cuzco proper, and also of Machu Picchu. Pisac, in the matchless perfection of its stone-cutting and its unvarying right angles (except in the beautiful circular walls around the holy altar of the intihuatana), its vertical walls and general plan, is in a class by itself; but the fitting and joining of the stones is identical with that of Sacsahuaman.

The impression made by Sacsahuaman is of an expenditure of labor out of proportion to results accomplished; that of a hugeness and weight beyond the requirements even of a fortress. So in Cuzco itself, there are Cyclopean walls and impregnable foundations without the superstructure even of a roof, except one of thatch. There was a tremendous expenditure of effort and a perfection of detail in work which seemed more or less irrational, an art which grew rankly but never flowered.

With all of its beauty of detail and tremendous strength the architecture of the Peruvian Ayars was somber. It was the product of a people who had evolved a culture of industrial peace and had been forced into defensive war. Their ancestors had worshipped a god of war; and some branches of their family cultivated a religion of blood, slaughter, human sacrifices, and cannibalism from which they themselves had not wholly escaped, but they had long since attained the conception of an omnipotent but benign Creator. Even their temples and palaces, with few exceptions blank walls without an opening or relief save an occasional doorway, seemed all like fortresses against dreaded attack, and possibly were intended as such. This oppressive thought may possibly have shaped and stifled the architectural genius of the Ayar-Incas and their predecessors.

VI

BEYOND THE "RODADERO"

JUST across the level approach to the north of Sacsahuaman is the *Rodadero*, a hummock of soft limestone,
shaped like the top of a flattened dome, and polished
perfectly smooth by glacial action. Near its summit,
facing the fortress and overlooking the level parade-
ground lying between, is carved, with great precision and
perfect alignment, a square and perfectly level emplacement or pedestal; and a series of several such levels,
similarly cut, falls away down the slope of the rock to
the right and left like a flight of broad, low steps. Rising
behind, and forming a back to the series, the rock is cut
into a smooth perpendicular. A similar series, a step
lower, lies in front of these, and still lower in front of
the second series of steps there are several larger emplacements more deeply but not so smoothly cut.

Back of these well-proportioned and beautifully carved
broad flat steps, the rock rises a foot or two higher to its
gently rounded summit, and towards the front and sides
falls sharply away down its dome-like slopes. Those
classically cut emplacements are often spoken of as the
"Inca's throne," or the "seat of the Inca," from which he
watched the progress of the stupendous work a few yards
away. But the carvings bear no resemblance to seats, and
would be too uncomfortable for the seats even of an Inca
and his court. It is much more likely that they were

pedestals for idols placed to keep watch over the work which was no doubt conducted with solemn religious rites, and before which ceremonials and sacrifices were offered. Such great rocks in many places were used as open-air altars and sanctuaries. The level field in front, aside from its military advantage, was no doubt a drill-ground for the evolutions of soldiers,—a place of games and athletic exercises, and possibly also used as a theater for the enactment of dramas and pageants.

To the north the country rises in rolling blue-grass hills, refreshed with frequent springs of cold, clear water. Some of these in ancient times were conveyed to distant slopes in well-constructed ditches and aqueducts that are still in good condition. In many of these old conduits pleasant brooks are still flowing. It is a pleasant land, bathed in the brilliant but not oppressive summer sun. It may well have been chosen as the royal seat of the rulers of an empire. It is a limestone country of fertile soil, favorable to the growing of fat cattle and horses of good fettle.

As one rides over the pleasant slopes a yellow-breasted quail,—seeming to prefer a solitary life and not living in coveys like the Virginia partridge,—thunders up from his feet; or a small nide of brown *perdices* whir swiftly around the point of a slope or hillock. These native pheasants are short-tailed, clean-legged, trim-looking birds, with the beautifully penciled brown shadings and markings of their family; and it is said the natives run them down with dogs as they rise only twice and after that are incapable of flight for the time being. But, nevertheless, in their remote hills where firearms and

IDOL PEDESTALS OF THE HUACA

Sacred high-place of the so-called Rodadero, facing the fortress of Sacsahuaman.

SACRED STONE OF SAYACUSCA, NEAR CUZCO
Note the carved idol seats.

sportsmen are seldom seen, these native Andean species
have survived the Indian and the Spaniard, and in some
places are still quite plentiful.

North of Sacsahuaman and the *Rodadero* are many
limestone ledges and megaliths. As in most limestone
countries there are many caves, grottoes, and underground
passages. Many of these subterranean galleries have been
extended by the ancient inhabitants, and there are various
stories of their secret ramifications and connections with
Cuzco and other points in the vicinity. They have not
been fully explored. Many of the caves and grottoes
were handsomely carved, and were used as the sepulchers
of the rich and noble in pre-Spanish times.

A short distance from the *Rodadero* two limestone
megaliths have been handsomely carved into great seats or
thrones, possibly for the rest or recreation of the Inca, in
this pleasant retreat above the city. They stand near the
sacred stone of Sayacusca, with its carved altar-place, idol-
pedestals, and priests' seats. On one side of this great
carved boulder the approaching cliffs almost completely
shut off a secluded, almost secret place, no doubt useful
in the pagan ritual of the priests. The great flat altar
was on the summit of the rock, and on the outer side, at
its base a leveled space, no doubt a theater of public ceremonial and worship.

VII

TAMPU MACHAY

SOME miles further back, over the open ridges towards the north in a beautiful, grass-covered glen, without trees,—for it is a treeless country, though no doubt there are many species which would grow there if planted,—are the royal baths, tomb, and open temple of Tampu Machay. The streams of pure water, drawn from secret sources in hidden conduits, are still flowing out in the beautifully fluted grooves,—a bit of the active life of the place which still survives, and seems to speak in the cheerful murmur of the waters of the continuity of the past, of kings and nobles, of a rude luxury and pagan rites: scenes of which this active, living fountain was a part.

The fountains flow through a succession of carved channels in limestone rocks over the brinks of two low terraces, retained by low walls of cut stones,—rising one above the other to a high wall of magnificent masonry of dressed stones laid somewhat irregularly, but perfectly joined. This plain but impressive wall façade is about seventy-five feet long and ten feet high,—lower at one end which is thrown forward into a flanking wing. A short but impressive stairway of cut stones of large size leads up between the wing and the main wall to the principal terrace, through a plain but superb gateway with typical inclined sides narrowing towards the top. Nothing could exceed the simple beauty of the masonry

Grooved channels in which the water still flows in the sacred fountain of the prehistoric temple-tomb of Tampu-Machay.

Photograph by the author.

TAMPU-MACHAY

The proportion can be noted by the group of horses in the background.

of this wing, with its buttressed corners, and angles of unbroken stone.

In the face of the solidly built wing is a handsome doorway,—its entablature supported by a beautifully laid lintel of a single stone. This doorway is sealed by great cut stones, closely fitted into its embrasure, and apparently has never been opened. It is probably the tomb of an emperor. Above the walls of the wing and to the right, as one ascends the stone steps, is a level terrace, faced and backed with masonry walls. Whether a hidden chamber lies beneath this, no effort has been made to determine. The stairway also leads to a longer terrace on the left, back of which stands another wall of exquisite masonry. This is composed of large stones, handsomely cut and regularly laid, and contains four large niches, with characteristic inclined sides and impressive entablature supported on well-laid monolithic lintels.

The sacred structure is an open-air temple and bath,— perhaps also a tomb. Back of it lies the higher hillside, while in front the slope runs steeply down to a small and grassy ravine. In its complete seclusion, its excellent workmanship, its plain but well-proportioned lines, its freedom from ornament, and its openness to the nature which its builders worshipped, it has an exquisite, pagan beauty.

VIII

OLLANTAYTAMBO

SOME five miles below the mouth of the Chospiyoc, the Marcacocha, a clear cold creek, comes into the Vilcanota from the north through a lovely small valley lying at right angles to that of the larger stream. At the point some half-mile from the river where the Marcacocha passes out from the hills which enclose it, into the valley of the Vilcanota, is the prehistoric village of Ollantay-tambo, still inhabited by the descendants of its mysterious builders.

Some sixty feet up on the point of the western one of the two promontories between which the stream flows into the Sacred Valley, is the unfinished open temple of Ollantaytambo,—its construction interrupted by the flight of its ancient builders from some ruthless conqueror or their destruction long before the rise to power of the Incas. It is generally called a fortress; but while there are fortresses of a similar matchless stone masonry where the Vilcanota valley narrows some miles below at Salapunco, also at Sacsahuaman, and elsewhere in the vicinity, and while the marvelous "high-place" of Ollantaytambo is in a position of strength, protected by an adobe wall behind, by its precipitous natural approaches on the east and south, its high terraces and parapets on the north, it still was but a holy place and sacrificial altar. Like others of the great sanctuaries of these and other early peoples,—for instance, the altars of Bethel and Beersheba or the Parthenon itself on its Acropolis,—it was built on a high place.

At the foot of the precipitous rock on which the sanctuary stands lies the ancient village,—its immemorial streets and stone houses still occupied by the remnants of the indigenous people. The small but full-flowing stream of water runs through the town, kept within its banks by ancient walls of solid masonry. The houses, many centuries old, are built partly of rough and partly of smoothly cut stone,—one story high, with attics, and windows in the gable ends.

The people, like the North American Indian, have the copper color of the Mongolian when continually exposed to the weather. They are sturdy and well-built. As elsewhere among primitive people the women do much of the work. The dress of the women is a short, tight-fitting jacket scarcely reaching the waist, and a short skirt or a number of skirts reaching scarcely to the knee. The men wear short jackets, short trousers and hats much like those worn by Chinese coolies. As they look up from their work in the field at a passer-by one is struck by their resemblance to Chinese farm laborers.

As at Cuzco, the streets, enclosed by the ancient walls, are very narrow, some of them scarcely six feet wide. The vale of the Marcacocha widens above the village and is carefully cultivated, its level fields held in retaining walls in broad terraces, and irrigated through well-constructed ditches.

The great temple faces to the east where the sun-god casts his first morning rays through the gap of the Vilcanota. Back of the temple, beyond the grass-covered ridges, rise in full view the sublime snowy heights of the peak of Chicón, 19,342 feet above the sea. The town immediately at the base of the temple, the Marcacocha valley to the north between its high mountains, the plain of Vilcanota to the east and west, the great stone aqueducts, the terraced fields, lay spread beneath the sacred place like a panorama.

The Vilcanota here flows with a powerful current and in times of flood is a raging torrent, but for many miles wherever it was likely to break down its banks and damage the carefully built up gardens along its shores, it was restrained by powerfully constructed stone walls so well built that notwithstanding the force of the floods of many centuries, and long neglect, these walls still stand and serve their ancient purpose. Similar evidences of the industry, skill, and energy of the ancient Peruvian tribes are found in the retaining walls on the banks of the Sonche River near Chachapoyas in northern Peru, and in other widely scattered localities.

From the high-place all the actions of the people could be observed,—their work in the fields, their movements in the pueblo, their entry and leaving of their houses were all under the scrutiny of the priests at the temple above.

At the base of the hill, near the series of terraces leading up to the great altar are handsomely cut stones of considerable size, as though prepared for an edifice never begun. Near by is the basin of the "Inca's Baths," supplied with water flowing through carved stone conduits. Dwellings larger and handsomer than the rest stand, partly in ruins, close to the base of the sacred cliff,— the former residences of chiefs or persons of distinction.

DETAIL OF PREHISTORIC VILLAGE OF OLLANTAYTAMBO

Note the stone conduit for the stream which flows through the town.

THE FIVE WALLED TERRACES OF THE TEMPLE OF
OLLANTAYTAMBO

The "high-place" and unfinished altar is above the wall with the niches.

Photograph by the author.

In a recess or small hollow in the mountain base, adjoining the rocky promontory on which the temple is built, is a series of agricultural terraces sustaining gardens constructed for the especial use of the priests of the sanctuary. These gardens are now dry and desolate but were no doubt formerly watered from sources now lost.

Two sides of the jutting cliff of shale on which the high altar is placed are perpendicular and impassable; the third, which is also steep but less so than the others, is solidly walled up in a massive series of terraces and ramparts of cut and dressed stone,—the blocks perfectly fitted together without mortar and inclined slightly inward after the manner of Cuzco. The narrow flat terraces lie at the bases of the successive walls and afford a series of balconies or promenades leading up to the "high-place" above. The two upper walls are of more massive stones, more smoothly cut, and evenly faced. In the last, and highest as well as the most massive and highly finished rampart, just underneath the bulge of the natural rock which rises above the façade, and furnishes the final approach to the holy place itself, is a series of ten niches, each some two feet in height, perfectly aligned, mathematically spaced, of beautiful proportions, cut with the utmost perfection of the stone-mason's art. These were for the idols of the temple.

The art though pagan is classic in its splendid simplicity, heightened in its beauty by its immediate blending with nature itself. The perfect walls of masonry, their severity broken by the chaste and harmonious niches in the highest tier, seem a part of the ruggedness of the cliff itself, which, as in the great temples of Machu Picchu and Pisac, rises above the magnificent masonry in the untouched and savage beauty of nature as the fit and impregnable altar of the holy place. The whole work, improving in its finish and beauty from the base towards the summit, seems to reach its superb climax and capital in the enduring mold of the mountains. It speaks aloud the passionate love of nature of its builders, who left, to crown their supreme effort, the great rock itself.

Stone steps lead from the ground at the base to the first terrace. Proceeding on this to the left, along the base of the second wall to where it is reduced in height, one obtains an ascent to the terrace above. After passing along this to the right around the corner of the masonry, one finds steps which lead up by the end of the third wall to another series of steps leading up through a square-cut gateway in the fourth wall to the long high esplanade running at the base of the fifth and uppermost wall, which contains the series of niches. In the west end of this wall an open doorway, of classic proportion and simplicity of design with "reentry" lintels and jambs inclined inwards, after the usual type of ancient Peru, opens from the esplanade to a passage over the natural rock of the cliff to the highest point in the temple,—the supreme place of worship and sacrifice.

A row of six huge, polished, red porphyry slabs, placed on end, joined together by narrow stones of the same kind so perfectly fitted that,—though centuries have passed over them since from some sudden terror or disaster the great work was interrupted and left in an unfinished state,—there is no visible opening between them. They are placed with their backs to a perpendicular wall cut down in the natural stone in the cliff which rises steadily towards the mountains behind it,—its top at the point of the cut slightly more than flush with the tops of the monumental slabs. The top line of this polished stone altar-wall is irregular,—as the stones composing it vary a few inches in length. The base line is also uneven and does not rest upon the ground except at the ends, and is supported on smaller stones placed here and there as temporary piers while the great slabs were being fitted into place.

These irregularities would undoubtedly have disappeared, covered by a carved base stone and a stone coping, had the great structure been completed. The unevenness of the base line would possibly have been covered by the great altar stone itself forming the floor of the holy place and fitting close against the base of the upright slabs. As left, in the strange interruption of the marvelous work,— left in the crudeness of its unfinished state, but far enough advanced to display forever the genius of its architects and masons,—only the bare ground is the floor of the altar. No doubt some of the so-called "tired stones," abandoned on the way from the quarry to the temple,—one of which is twenty-one feet six inches long, fifteen feet wide, and while partly embedded exposing five feet of thickness above the ground,—were to have constituted the floor of the altar, to have been joined to the base of the upright slabs.

The art of the builders of the temple of Ollantaytambo was not only exquisite in the combined grandeur and simplicity of its conception but exalted in its display of a command of the exact science of equilibrium, of balanced weights, and in the mathematical perfection of its complicated alignment. As stated above, the structure, though composed of six stones of tremendous weight and size, does not rest directly upon the ground except at the extremities; nor is it immediately supported by the native rock at its back. There is a space of some eighteen inches between the majestic porphyry wall and the native rock behind it,—and yet the structure, even in its unfinished state, has stood for an unknown number of centuries, perhaps forty, without losing even by an imperceptible degree the plumb and equilibrium in which its great builders placed it. Notwithstanding its tremendous weight, it gives such an impression of lightness as to almost seem to be suspended in the air. Open at the bottom and with a free space at the back, it would seem to be without adequate support. The largest of the six stones of which the structure is composed, the one at the right end, is 11.5 feet in height, 7.1 feet wide at the base, 6.4 feet wide at the top, and 5.9 feet thick.[1] The smallest stone, the third from the right, is 12.8 feet long, 3.7 feet wide at the base, 4.2 feet wide at the top, and 2.3 feet thick.

These great stones are so shaped and placed that the very weight of the stones, balanced one against another, operates by the constant force of gravity to bind them to each other as though they were but one stone instead of several. By the genius of the builders the six great stones, and the several smaller ones which constitute and fill the

---

[1] Measurements made by Ephraim George Squier, given on page 501 of his interesting work, *Peru: Incidents of Travel and Exploration in the Land of the Incas.*

UNFINISHED HIGH ALTAR, TEMPLE OF OLLANTAYTAMBO

Photograph by M. Mancilla.

joints between them, become, in the solidity of their emplacement, as one solid rock. Though the true arch is generally supposed to be unknown in prehistoric Peruvian architecture, the essential principle of the arch, whether flat or curved, is exhibited in the utmost perfection of execution in this splendid antique structure of the Vilcanota. As the two end stones of this magnificent wall are sufficiently braced and anchored, the wall would stand unmoved even if all supports should be removed from underneath the other four. In other words, it would span, as a solid stone beam, a chasm 21.1 feet wide, or serve as a lintel over the doorway of some vast cathedral.[2]

The device which gives the structure its impregnable solidity is the principle of the keystone of an arch. The six stones are divided into three sets of two stones each. The unit composed of the two on the left is 9.8 feet wide at the top and 10.9 feet wide at the bottom,—a spread from top to base of 1.1 feet. The unit composed of the two stones at the right end of the wall is similarly shaped; being 13.2 feet wide at the top and 14.1 at the bottom, a spread of .9 foot. A part of this difference is taken up by the lean of the end lines of the wall towards the center; but the space between the two end units is the shape of a wedge-socket, into which, as a bolt into a nut, the wedge-shaped unit of the two inner stones,—10.2 feet

[2] Actually some of the inner stones are without basic support; and the great end slabs are held in position, bound to the foundation, by being shaped so that the thrust upon them of the weight of the structure is vertical rather than horizontal. The tremendous weight of the inner stones is perpendicular upon the inclined sides of the outer, tending rather to hold them in place than to dislodge them. In addition, their wedge-shaped outer base-corners are locked into scotches in the living rock of the cliff itself, so that the greater the weight and pressure upon them, the more immovably they are fixed.

wide at the top and 9.4 at the bottom, besides the thin
stone joints,—fits with mathematical exactness and locks
the massive structure into a compact and immovable
whole.

The smaller stones forming the joints are cut in exact
conformity with the larger ones into which they fit. The
actual strength and durability of the structure, as well as
the impression of solidity which its form excites, is enhanced by another use of the law of gravity and the great
weight of the stones themselves,—not only by the typical
slant inwards of the ends of the great wall, in the line of
the wall, but by the tilt of the entire plane of the wall
from the perpendicular, back towards its supports in the
living rock.

There is a suggestion of the Egyptian in the red porphyry, and in the temple's massiveness, solidity, and
sloping sides. This impressive entablature, evidently
the back wall of an unfinished temple of the sun, is 34.4
feet long at the base and 33.2 on the top line. The small
contraction of the whole from the base to the top,—of 1.2
feet,—though it might seem negligible, is powerfully
effective.[3]

As in all the ancient works of Peru the art of their
makers is shown as much by the magnificence of location
and the grandeur of its outlook as in the excellence of

---

[3] It is a curious circumstance that in rather dim outline, but plainly
to be seen when closely examined, there is down the center line of the
center stone in the wall,—the fourth from the left,—a series of three conventional geometric figures, four-sided diamonds in relief, each side in-
dented by several angles,—corresponding with the same design in intaglio
on stones among the ruins of Tiahuanaco. This identical design is likewise to be observed in the ornamentation of aboriginal gold axes discovered
near Chordeleg in Ecuador. See illustration in *The Gold Treasure of
Sigsig*, by Marshall H. Saville, Heye Foundation, p. 16.

the work itself. Sixty feet above the plain and village at its base, overlooking the terraced fields spread in matchless perfection of successive levels, divided by the straight lines of their retaining walls and aqueducts in the valley below,—a pleasing prospect of agricultural art,—the high altar faces up the river valley and looks through the great gap of the river directly to the east. The sun,—worshipped by the builders of this temple as a deity in itself and as the highest material personification of the unseen creator of the world,—appearing in the notch between the great mountain bulwarks of the river, casts its first morning rays full upon the polished wall of the high-place. In the other direction, the servitors of the temple, as they faced the holy altar, saw the sun sink behind the gilded and empurpled snows and glaciers of Chicón. To the south, across the swift Vilcanota, the great bare ridges of the cordillera rise to enormous heights. The river, whose general direction is to the north, here flows west, but soon loses its course in the convolutions of its mighty gorge. The vale of Marcacocha, with its irrigated fields, opens pleasantly to the north,—its cold stream flowing at the base of the great temple and fructifying the valley below.

A considerable area in the rear of the temple is enclosed in a high wall of adobe and stone covered with a yellow plaster of such excellent quality that it retains its color and texture unimpaired after centuries of exposure and neglect. The wall with excellent plumb and alignment runs for a considerable distance up the steep hillside. A narrow coping or cornice gives it a finished appearance. It was intended, of course, for the privacy and protection of the priests whose houses stood within the enclosure and is generally, as the temple itself, referred to as a fortress. As a matter of fact, from the steep hillside above the wall can be easily scaled. The foundations and ruins of the priests' houses are still within the enclosure, with the terraced gardens now dry and deserted alongside. High up on the shoulder of the ridge above the great temple stands a well-constructed mausoleum,—its mummy-niches empty, the doors long since torn away from the lock-holds provided for them in the stones.

Across the valley of the Marcacocha, high up on the precipitous mountain-side to the northeast, stands a large house built in a succession of tiers adapted to its steep location,—said to have been the home of the sacred virgins. The ruins of the Inca's palace stand in the valley near the river. A beautifully cut stone bath-seat, with holes for staves to support the canopy which protected from the sun the queen or noble who used it, still lies in place in the edge of the river by a pleasant pool,—the waters purling against it just as in the time of its luxurious owner. A prehistoric bridge,—with its megalithic piers, which by the very weight of the stones of which they are constructed, placed in position with precision and regularity, have withstood the torrents of many centuries,—still supports a swinging superstructure, as in the days of the Incas and their remote predecessors.

IX

THE QUARRY AND INCLINED WAY

THE great red stones of the temple of Ollantaytambo were brought from a quarry some six miles distant,—on the opposite side of the river, 3,000 feet up the mountain-side. The splendid altar stands 60 feet above the village at its base and at least 300 feet above the river at the point at which the megaliths were brought across some two miles down the stream. Quarried at the base of a porphyritic cliff, towering above the quarry itself 6,000 feet, the stones were cut and polished on long ter-races supported by walls of masonry of massive strength, so constructed,—the walls inclining towards the face of the mountain for greater powers of resistance,—as to receive the tremendous crude slabs as they were quarried off from the face of the high dike, or selected from those which had been broken off in more or less regular form by the action of frost.

At points of vantage, on great stones above the quarry, small guard-houses,—huts in which the guards of gangs of slaves working in the quarry could find shelter from the weather and still observe the work,—are yet standing. With the unfinished blocks in all degrees of preparation lying about on the terrace, the ground strewn with chips cut from the rocks, it seems as though the work had but just been interrupted. It requires but little imagination to repeople the ancient scene. The guard-huts built and

roofed with stone remind one of the small shelters of more
flimsy material which one sees today in the same valley
of the Vilcanota and many other places in Peru, sometimes raised on a pole platform or placed on some natural
point of vantage from which a watchman can guard his
crops against thieves. Thrown from the terrace to the
slope below, the path of the descent of the monoliths to
the river is still clearly marked.

To move these tremendous slabs over the powerful
current of the river and carry them to the summit of the
rocky promontory several miles up the stream and three
hundred feet above it, would tax the resources of modern
science. That the prehistoric builders of the Vilcanota
were masters of the mechanics of weights and balances,
as of the geometry of form, is proved by the brilliant exhibition of their works. The mathematics of curves and
angles, of grade and proportion, was never exhibited in
greater perfection of application than in Cuzco, the massive altar of Ollantaytambo, the chaste temple of Pisac,
the magic city of Machu Picchu.

Along with the mastery of the science of form and the
fine art of the mason went the knowledge of mechanics,—
not exceeded at the present day in the field in which it was
applied. Especially the principles of the balancing of
weights and of the lever were understood and applied by
these megalithic builders. There is nowhere in the
world, perhaps, a more complete exhibition of the perfect
control and use of the force of gravity itself to counteract
the destructive power of gravity,—to hold and bind a
structure in its exact place,—than in the high altar of
Ollantaytambo; and yet, even with this complete mastery

of the mechanics of weights, it would have been impossible for the Quichua-Ayar builders of Peru to move the huge slabs of the temple of Ollantaytambo across a river and up a mountain but for their unlimited control of manpower.

From the level of the river valley an inclined way of the most gradual and easiest grade was constructed to the temple-site. This great way more than half a mile in length, solidly built, walled in with rock, is still plainly to be seen. Upon rollers, with great levers, with tackle of unbreakable strength, and timbers held in place by knobs left upon the slabs for that purpose,—and still remaining even on the otherwise polished face of the altar, —thousands of slaves under the command of a despot moved the great rocks over the river upon a bridge which must have been low and of prodigious strength, across the valley up the inclined way to the holy place, where the master builders set them in a structure which, though they had no written language, will carry the record of their art into the incalculable future.

But calamity, sudden and terrible disaster, fell upon them. Caught in the very midst of their work, they quit upon the instant, while it was in the very flush of progress, as though their arms lifted with the chisel and hammer had been stricken down by the sword. All about the quarry lie stones in every degree of manufacture and great finished sills and cornices lie strewn about the altar itself, not yet put in place. Here and there along the way between the quarry and the temple finished stones were left, dropped in the very movement. Lying there today as they have lain for ages, they bring back the scene as though it were but yesterday. The greatest of them all lies on the inclined way not far from the destination it never reached. Near it is the abandoned *green stone* of sacrifice, like that in the temple of Huitzilopochtli in the city of Mexico.

The mule caravans bringing tropical fruits and coca from Santa Ana pass by it; but the mule-drivers, degraded descendants of a race which had the genius, energy, and organization to accomplish so great a work, scarcely give it a passing glance. As ignorant and indifferent to their past as they are hopeless of their future, with a note of pathos and poetry they call these great plinths of the altar, resting there for centuries along the arduous way, the "tired stones,"—as though typical of their race itself, cut off in its progress, exhausted in the struggle. Like the "tired stones" they are sleeping along the way to the temple.

X

TERRACED FARMS

AT strategic points above Ollantaytambo, where ridges from the mountains come down close to the river, there are ruins of massive fortresses on both banks of the stream which guard this section of the valley from invasion in that direction. Protected in its lovely and quiet valley, this branch of the great Mexican-Mayan race, under a new leadership and control, developed its restricted but rich and powerful domain to the highest possible extent. In its exquisite valley it carried intensive agriculture to as high a point as it ever reached.

Where it was advantageous to do so, the turbulent river was straightened and confined within stone walls. Large portions of the valley were graded in series of level terraces, supported by stone walls in some places fifteen feet in height, with the typical inward slope, of stones of varying sizes fitted well together in perfect alignment and in many places smoothed on the outer surface. At frequent intervals steps formed by series of stones with projecting ends enabled the ancient farmers to pass from terrace to terrace.

The space behind the walls was filled in first with small stones and earth, on the top of which was placed a level surface of rich soil brought from the alluvium of near-by slopes. All was the product of hand labor, operating under the military control of autocratic socialism. Stupendous results were obtained with apparent ease from the steady, continuous, patient, scientifically directed labor of the entire working community. Water was brought from the small streams which abounded in the near-by hills, fed by ample rains and the melting snows and glaciers which covered the higher peaks. Perfectly graded ditches with stone aqueducts at the crossing of ravines, and tunnels through obstructing rock, led to splendid terraces where the water was conveyed from one to another by a well-arranged system of conduits.

The potato and tomato were indigenous; maize, yielding so marvelously in the middle valleys of the Andes, had been brought from the north in the earliest migrations. Many new varieties of it had been developed in its new environment, including the diminutive species which ripens at an altitude of 12,800 feet on the "Island of the Sun" and in the valleys opening upon Lake Titicaca. The Vilcanotans traded with the Anti-suyus, in the "hot lands" below, for coca, bananas, timber, and nuts. Their herds of llamas and alpacas grazed on the vast ranges to the snow-line on the cordilleras which towered above them and stretched away in a vast perspective in every direction.

Running through the valley was a carefully graded and, in places, paved road. It was thoroughly drained and the waters are still running in the old subterranean culverts. Far down the valley at various places where the road passes over ledges of rock the steps cut in the solid stone are still in use.

Some sixteen miles below Ollantaytambo, at Havaspampa, the valley narrows and the mountains close in again upon the river. At this point, where there is scarcely room for the passage of the road on the brink of the steep gorge cut by the river in the granite ridge, Salapunco, a fortress of tremendous strength, commands approach from above. It is located on the right bank of the river and covers a considerable area. Like each of the great structures of ancient Peru, it is distinctive in character; and while its masonry is of the same general type as that of the entire region, its plan and the details of its construction are different. It is built of large trapezoid granite blocks of graded size and uniform shape, evenly placed and exactly fitted without mortar.

A long impregnable rampart from twelve to fifteen feet in height, varying with the slope of the ground, with a characteristic slant inwards, faces the river. The ancient road passes along its base. A sally-port of moderate dimensions, with inclined sides and monolithic lintel, leads from vaulted chambers and parapets above. The esplanade of the fortress is now overgrown with grass and bushes,—but its splendid masonry, though abandoned for centuries, is still in perfect condition. In one of the outer angles of the great wall under a flimsy shelter, a roadway blacksmith's shop serves the needs of travelers and of the railroad work going on near by. In another corner of the great wall a miserable outdoor school, with a wan-looking teacher, gives scant instruction to a few anemic pupils,—in hopeless contrast with the genius and virility which constructed the mighty fort in whose shadow they drone their meager lessons, unconscious of their race's past.

Below this point, in the deeper and more stupendous gorges of the granite mountains, ancient home of this pre-Inca prehistoric race of master masons, on the summit of a rocky promontory held in a loop of the river, almost surrounded by its mighty cañon, is the strange deserted city of Machu Picchu. Forced out of the valley above by successive war-like irruptions of fierce and hostile kinsmen, these great builders had found a pleasant abiding place lower down the valley.

The river falls rapidly and tropical forests begin to crowd upon its banks and swarm up the adjacent mountain-sides. The swift current winds in tremendous turnings through the cordillera Vilcanota, cutting its gorge to the very base of the granite barriers. The heat is tempered by the great fields of snow and ice above and yet it is a land of sun and flowers, calm in the hospitable shelter of the cathedral-like walls fashioned by the river itself. Game, fish, and fruits are plentiful, and the forests are cheerful with the music and gorgeous colors of many birds.

With the labor of their own people or of conquered slaves, the leaders of the ancient race who penetrated into this far and deep recess of the Andes left imperishable proofs, not only of their power but of their enlightened mastery of certain branches of industrial art. Under the overhanging boughs of dense tropical forests, where the dark, swift waters seem to run in untouched, primeval wildness, a careful observation shows massive embankments of vertical walls of cut and fitted stone still defining the limit of the torrent and protecting the border of what

GORGE OF THE MIDDLE VILCANOTA

Photograph by the author.

were once intensely cultivated fields,—centuries since reverted to a wilderness.

Where the hills open into the cañons of flush tributary creeks bringing their waters from the heart of the mountain mass, there can yet be found, here and there far back on their upper courses, dams built by the ancient race. Along the slope of the cañon sides are the long lines of aqueducts which led the waters of the glacier-fed streams to elaborate series of walled terraces on the open lands about the quebrada mouths,—where the most intense cultivation of the soil with constant refertilization and the application of water at will to the growing crops, produced upon small areas food for many people. Some of the terraces in this section of the Vilcanota, in finish, in the care and perfection of their construction,—in many places with smoothed stones,—and in the mastery of natural obstacles, surpass any others in Peru.

Near the fort of Salapunco, for the convenience, no doubt, of its garrison, walls of splendid workmanship retaining narrow terraces only a few feet in width, rise one almost on top of another from the river's edge to the road. The ancient paved road of the valley is still in use here,—traffic by mule and burro passing back and forth upon it between the rich but isolated tropical valley of Santa Ana, far down the great river, and the present terminus of the narrow-gauge railroad at Ollantaytambo.[1]

Ancient stone buildings stand here and there along the

[1] The old Inca road had disappeared in places where the river had undermined the steep slopes on which it was built; and travel into the Santa Ana was very difficult until these gaps were repaired by the Government and the broken portions of the old road replaced by a rather crude new mule trail.

way, and storehouses, halls, temples, convents, and pris-
ons are clustered about ancient agricultural centers,—
elaborate systems of terraces so well built that though
deserted they are still in an excellent state of preservation,
—where the smaller branch valleys widen into that of
the Vilcanota.

XI

PISAC

Above Ollantaytambo,—after narrowing to a pass where ribs of the mountain ranges run down to the river at the site of the ancient forts which protected Ollantaytambo on the south,—the Sacred Valley widens again into the lovely vale of Yucay. For a distance of more than thirty miles the river here flows west. Its channel has been straightened,—confined in many places between the masonry walls of the prehistoric builders. Its rocky bed where it had spread over the valley has been filled in with rich soil,—graded, leveled, and retained in place by stone walls still in perfect alignment, with the characteristic inward slope; projecting stone steps give easy passageway from one level to another. Aqueducts brought water from the adjacent mountains, and the fructifying stream was conveyed in small rills from terrace to terrace by conduits so arranged as to prevent the washing of the soil.[1]

[1] At Urcos, between Ollantaytambo and Pisac, a Presbyterian Mission operates an hacienda where the Indians are taught improved methods of farming and the mechanic arts, such as weaving, shoe-making, and carpentry. The hacienda is located in one of the most beautiful spots of the valley and is unusually well supplied with water.

The legend is that it was once the home of a famous Inca general. He had a beautiful daughter and two young Inca Princes were desperately in love with the girl. She was unable or unwilling to decide between them.

Her father's land was suffering for the lack of water. Year after year his crops were cut short by the drought and there appeared to be no way

On the floor of the valley, where the slope is gentle, the fields,—marked by dividing lines of stone aqueducts and retaining walls,—are of considerable size, the dividing-walls generally running at right angles to the river. Near the base of the hills where the foot of some ridge extends into the plain, terrace-walls of graceful and complex curves, conforming to the slope, parallel each other, supporting beautiful formal gardens of narrowing successive terraces as the steeper mountain-side is approached. Back of these in clumps of trees, overlooking the valley with its terraced gardens and facing the panorama of the cordillera on the opposite side of the river, snowy peaks gleaming in the distance, are the ruins of princely Inca residences. Here and there in favorable locations the steep bases of the hills themselves are terraced up in narrow but delightful gardens, with series of walls running parallel to the river.

Near where the branch valley of the Cachimayo, which comes down from Cuzco, debouches into that of the Vilcanota, the peak of Pisac rises some two thousand feet above the river which flows about its base. It stands out

in which water could be obtained. Finally the young girl told the Princes that she would marry the one who would supply the land with water.

The older of the two Princes with an army of laborers placed a dam in the river far above and by a long ditch brought water to the hacienda; but when the season of drought came the water ceased to flow in the ditch and the maize wilted.

The younger Prince went to a never-failing lake high up in the mountains to the north and, with the force of workmen which he controlled, cut a channel through the rocky crest of the ridge which shut it off from the valley, so that a stream of water fell in a cascade over the precipice. He then conveyed the stream by a ditch to the hacienda, providing an ample supply of water for the land throughout the year.

The beautiful girl kept her word and married the handsome young Prince; and the hacienda has ever since been celebrated as the best watered of all those in the valley.

from the higher mountains of the Paucartambo range, back of it to the northeast, like a huge flying buttress. An ancient village, partly Spanish-colonial and partly Inca or Quichua,—a large adobe church and plaza in the center, —lies at the foot of the peak, on the north bank of the stream. A huge ficus (so-called fig, but in appearance more like a beech) tree with wide-spreading branches and dense foliage stands in the plaza. The lovely vale of the Chongo spreads about the eastern base of the peak and rises gradually to the northeast towards the pass which leads over the snowy cordillera to the Paucartambo. The clear creek which waters this valley is perennially fed by the snows of the sierras and empties into the Vilcanota River just above the Inca town.

A little below, and on the opposite side of the river, a narrow gorge, through which a tumbling cascade falls, widens out as it approaches the plain of the river. A well-traveled mule and llama trail affords a short-cut to Cuzco up this gorge and over the grass-covered limestone hills. Through the winding course of this cañon there are many ruins of Quichua *andenes*, or terraces, in the rich alluvial soil along the base of the steep hills on either side, well watered by small ditches easily graded here and there and fed from little diversion dams in the tumbling brook falling rapidly down the quebrada. One of these dams, almost escaping notice as one rides by, marks the source of a ditch which continues far up on the mountain-side, curves around the angled buttress flanking the mouth of the quebrada, and carries its stream in a line of perfect grade for miles along the high slopes to terraces far up the river. A short distance up the rapidly rising trail, a rock and a slight embankment of earth again diverts a part of the mountain stream into another ditch,—parallel to the former but higher up the mountain, leading to other terraced gardens still further up the Vilcanota.

Down in the quebrada, sheltered from the winds, are at intervals Indian hamlets straggling along the banks and crossing, with rude bridges, the never-failing rivulet, —where the descendants of the immemorial peoples who constructed the great works in the valley below live their isolated lives. They tend their sheep and llamas on the ranges above, cultivate in a crude way patches of ground on the steep hillsides, and spin from primitive spindles their handfuls of wool as they move along the trails or over the ranges, fostering their aloofness, cherishing some dim conception of their ancestral legends, nurturing a gloomy resentment of their oppression.

A sharp cove leading back into a narrow gorge cuts into the northern flank of the peak of Pisac; so that the templed hill stands out like a ramparted promontory between the recess of the cove and the Chongo Valley on the other side. Much of the sides of the cove is faced and built up with walls of dressed stone with a typical slight inward slant, adjusted in straight lines or curves in harmony with the slopes of the hill, enclosing series of narrow terraces, in some places running far up towards the summits of the precipitous bastions around which they curve.

A long limestone stairway, with monolithic treads, leads up the steep crease of the cove, turning with many angles as its steep flights of steps mount towards the towers and temples on the high crest. A handsomely cut

ROUND TOWER FORTS ON POINT OF HEIGHT IN
FRONT OF TEMPLE OF PISAC

INTIHUATANA AND RUINS OF THE TEMPLE OF PISAC

Note the shadow cast by the sacred sun-dial. Chongo valley in right background.

Photograph by the author.

groove in the middle of the stairway formerly carried a little stream from the cleft above, which watered the climbing terraces and hanging gardens and now serves as excellent drainage. So perfectly were the stones laid some thousands of years ago, and so scientifically drained, that they have never been displaced by the decay and usage of the centuries. Today they are as when first constructed the passageway to the heights,—ringing to the blows of the iron-shod feet of our mules. They are a part of the famous ancient Inca road to the Paucartambo.

To the right and left the walled terraces rise, tier on tier, and on the very apex of the projecting peak a round stone tower overlooks the formal gardens, the curving terraces, and the silver line of the stone-diked river far below, stretching straight away down the lovely valley. Opposite, to the west, across the chasm of the Vilcanota, high up on the steep grass-covered mountain-sides, almost on a level with the high tower, are, distinctly marked, the long, straight parallel lines of ancient aqueducts and irrigation ditches. Near the foot of the towering fortress on the apex, built upon the steep slope towards the south and at other vantage points on jutting rocks, other round tower-like fortresses of stone command a view of the valley of the Chongo and the approaches in all directions,—the outworks and sentinel-towers of the holy place.

Ruins of buildings, residences perhaps of the guards and laborers of the temple,—overgrown with grass and cactus, masses of epiphytes hanging upon the tumbling walls,—cling to the declivities overlooking the Chongo Valley. Houses, stairways, villages, stick to the steep

sides of the bluffs; walls run down the crests of rock
ridges; terrace is piled on terrace of solid masonry clear
to the top of the jutting peak as though a whole mountain
had been walled in and converted into a mighty pyramid!
The natural rock cliffs where they had begun to crumble
away in places have been buttressed at their bases by the
retaining walls of the ancient builders.

Along the narrow ridge which joins the outstanding
peak, flanked with terraces and capped by its towers, with
the mountain mass behind, a path leads to the sacred
"high-place." Where the ridge widens a little a chaste
temple has been built about an outcropping basaltic rock.
On this round altar the intihuatana has been cut,—a part
of the living stone itself, which has been cut down and
leveled off around it so as to leave the sacred register of
the sun outstanding on the pinnacle of the rock.[2] Steps
cut in the stone lead up to the holy place. It is enclosed
in walls built of ashlar masonry of gray granite cut in
right angles, except where the angles are cut in conformity with a curve or inward inclination of the walls in some

[2] Dr. Horacio H. Urteaga says (*Boletín de la Sociedad Geográfica
de Lima*, XXIX (1913), 40) that the so-called intihuatanas were mere
hitching posts for sacrificial animals, and: "Despues de amarrar a la
res, juntandole las cuatro extremidades con una soga enlazada sujetaban
su cabeza á este punzón de piedra y de esta manera la aseguraban perfecta-
mente; en ese estado el degüello del animal se hacía sin dificultad."
He quotes Max Uhle as saying that the intihuatana of Pisac (giving its
latitude as 14° South) does not cast its shadow on the rock on which it
is situated when the sun is at the zenith except from April to September,
and so is not suitable as a sun-dial. Urteaga states that generally the
intihuatanas were covered by overhanging rocks which cut off the sun's
rays from them; and mentions several which were located in sepulchral
caves altogether hidden from the sun.
Dr. Uhle, if correctly quoted, seems to be mistaken as to the intihuatana
of Pisac. He apparently bases his calculations on a mistake as to its
dimensions,—stating its height to be twenty-eight cm. (11.0236 in.),—

places, with mechanical accuracy, smooth on all sides and laid together without mortar in the most exquisite perfection.

The intihuatana is approached by three terraces, through a typical doorway of slanting jambs and tasteful proportions. Platforms, retained and fronted by walls of cut granite, extend to great niched chambers of a temple and a palace. Back of these, towards the sierras, a Cyclopean retaining wall, twelve feet in height, supports an older place of ceremony, sixty by thirty feet in size, with an idol's pedestal cut with the utmost nicety in a great rock.

Far above, towards the snow-line of the mountains, other terraces can be seen. To the northwest the snows and glaciers of Chicón and Salcontay glisten in the sun, while below spreads the panorama of the walled and blooming valleys.

Here, as elsewhere among the ancient temples of the Andes, the profound appeal of the altar to the sun is greatly enhanced by the majesty of its setting. The sacred dial was open to the beams of light as they painted

while Squier, who personally measured it, gives its height as sixteen inches. Also its latitude is further north than 14° South,—about 13° 30′ S. It is exposed to the unobstructed rays of the sun at noontime throughout the year,—on the very summit of an open rock. The same is true of the great intihuatana of Machu Picchu. Dr. Urteaga's idea that these sacred objects, carefully guarded with elaborate walls of masonry, were mere hitching posts, would seem to be rather far-fetched. He does not explain how the process which he describes of tying the animal's head to the intihuatana in order to cut its throat, after its four feet had been roped together, could have been carried out in the burial caves where he locates many intihuatanas.

On the other hand, these objects having acquired a sacred symbolic character as guides of the people's action in relation with the sun, it was perfectly natural that conventional symbols of them should have been placed in tombs, for the service of the dead.

the beauties of morning on the snow peaks of the Vilcanota, and it marked the daily voyage of the sun until he sank behind them into the Pacific. It followed the great sun-god's movements around the Zodiac of the seasons, and pointed, as though with the finger of God himself, to the summer and the winter solstice. The matchless wall, with its classic doorway and terraced approaches, was, after all, but a roofless enclosure of the sacred stone. The perfection of the art of the masonry, the time and patience expended in the exquisite finish of mere walls, seemed to find their motive and high purpose as offerings to the holy place of the sun.

The builders who converted a mountain-side into a series of overhanging gardens, watered by scientifically constructed aqueducts, connected by stairways of stone, seemed to have no higher conception of architecture than walls with doorways and niches, though their masonry was as exquisite as that of the Taj Majal.

TEMPLE BUILT ABOUT THE SACRED SUN-DIAL AT PISAC

The sun-dial, or *intihuatana*, is the nubbin of natural rock rising just to the right of the center. Incidentally, note the Chinese-like hat, ancient style of the Vilcanota natives.

XII

MACHU PICCHU

And where hath vanished all their pomp and glory?
Who now can tell their deeds or even their name?
Ask these mute gods, who know the tragic story,
What is eternal fame.

       J. MACMILLAN BROWN, *The Riddle of the Pacific.*

THE extent and character of the prehistoric structures of the middle Vilcanota indicate that this delightful, secluded valley was held by the people which constructed them for a long period of time. Generations were required for their full development. Through diplomacy or force this well-organized people protected itself from the warlike and more savage indigenous tribes of the lower river valleys; and at the narrow gorge of the river below Havaspampa, at the great fort of Salapunco, they held in check the tribes from above.

But the day came when dire and ruthless disaster fell upon them. With terror they fled to the impregnable stronghold of Machu Picchu and there built a temple and the marvelous city which clustered around it on the very summit of a sharp ridge which looks down upon one side on a perpendicular precipice of 2,000 feet and is approached from the other side only by secret passages leading up the steep sides of the mountain. Like a Cyclopean moat around a mighty castle, the powerful and unfordable current of the Vilcanota enfolds the fortress city on

97

three sides in a mighty loop at the base of the granite cliffs. On the fourth side the easily defended peak of Machu Picchu, rising 3,900 feet above the river, stands across the way.[1]

Towering seven hundred feet above the city itself at the point of the promontory on which the city stands, enveloped in the bend of the river, rises the peak of Huayna Picchu. The path to its summit has not yet been discovered,[2] and yet, near its square and flattened summit of granite, can be seen, from the city, the straight, parallel jungle-covered lines of several huge terrace walls, no doubt supporting and serving a high altar.[3] From there, as from the ruined city itself, the view of the stupendous winding cañon of the river, the perspective of the sierras, range upon range, of lights playing upon the gigantic cliffs, and shadows falling over the abysses, of the airy line of snow ridges in the cloudy distance, the flaming clouds on the green sky of the horizon at the rising or the setting of the sun, make it a fit site for a temple and an altar to the God of Nature.

Strange platforms for sentinels hang out over the precipice to the west and here and there are small platforms of rocks indicating secret paths along the declivity. Across the sharp ridge there is a heavy stone wall between the city and the higher part of the peak of Machu Picchu.

[1] The river at the base of the western side of the Machu Picchu ridge is 6,400 feet above the sea. Hiram Bingham, *National Geographic Magazine*, April, 1913.

[2] Kenneth C. Heald, a member of Dr. Hiram Bingham's party of 1912, ascended it with tremendous difficulty by a hazardous route.

[3] Since the foregoing was written it has been reported from Peru that extensive prehistoric stone structures have been discovered on the summit of Huayna Picchu.

JUNGLE-GROWN SITE OF MACHU PICCHU AND
PEAK OF HUAYNA PICCHU

Great prehistoric ruins have recently been discovered on
the summit of this peak (upper right hand corner).

Photograph by the author.

POSTERN GATE IN THE WALL OF THE PREHIS-
TORIC CITY OF MACHU PICCHU

Photograph by the author.

This was the outer wall of the city, and between it and the inner wall a long series of stone embankments built with incredible patience and industry, as though the whole side of the mountain had been encased in artificial walls of stone, support narrow terraces where a few feet of soil was collected for cultivation. Lines of humble huts for the workers stand near by. Between these and the city was the inner wall with a trench or a "dry moat" at its base.

A gateway in this inner wall provides the only means of entering the city from this direction. This gate is remarkable for its monolithic lintel, the excellence of its masonry, the ingenious bolts and sockets cut into the stones of the jambs, and a stone ring, carved in one of the lintel stones, projecting above for the fastenings of the enclosure of the gateway.

The ridge on which the strange city is built runs north and south, rising into the peak of Machu Picchu close by to the south, and that of Huayna Picchu just beyond the city to the north. The entire ridge and the peaks are a solid mass of white granite with a thin covering of soil accumulated on certain slopes in which a rank growth of bamboos, vines, grasses and trees of considerable size grow in jungle-like profusion up to an elevation of 9,000 feet, with a thinner growth for three thousand feet or so further on.[4]

[4] Though this ancient city of the predecessors of the Incas was known to the modern Indians living in the vicinity, a family actually living on the site, it seems to have been unknown to all but a very few of the Spaniards or the white people of Peru until it was visited by Dr. Hiram Bingham in 1911. In 1912 he conducted an expedition to the site under the auspices of Yale University and the National Geographic Society, and the explorations are graphically described with a series of remarkable

The temples, the altars, the homes of the priests, the palaces of the Inca and the nobles, the convent of the virgins, are built along the narrow crest of the ridge overhanging the precipice to the west and the steeply sloping city to the east. On the highest point of the city, at the northern end of the ridge of temples and palaces, is the sacred sun-dial (inti-huatana) carved in a great rock. *Inti* means "sun"; *huatana*, "tie" or "band." The significance of the name, no doubt, is the tying up of the calendar of seasons and festivals, of agricultural work and social and religious functions, with the actual movement of the sun as automatically registered by the great dial.[5] By this means any lapses or irregularities in the computation were checked and corrected and the entire system kept

photographs of prehistoric ruins in the *National Geographic Magazine* for April, 1913. Dr. Bingham's party cleared away the jungle from the ruins and placed an ingenious temporary bridge over the swift Vilcanota River so that the city could be reached from the more accessible eastern side; but the bridge has long since been carried away by the floods and the rank jungle soon again covered the entire site and hid the white walls of the temples. When I visited the place in May, 1924, it was difficult to force one's way through the rank growth. I am told that in anticipation of a visit to the place in December, 1924, by General John J. Pershing,— which, however, did not materialize,—a new bridge was erected over the river (probably of a very temporary character) and some of the jungle cut away from the ruins.

Machu Picchu was marked on the map published by Sir Clements R. Markham in *The Incas of Peru* (London) in 1910. It was not mentioned, however, in the text. Father Humberto Suarez A., Chaplain of the Naval Academy of Peru, states that the ancient name of the city was Willcas-Marka (Sacred City) and that under this name it was referred to in the writings of Cieza de Leon, Herrera, and Antonio Raimondi. Father Humberto also states that this was the city of refuge of the last Incas, after the Spanish conquest. *Ciudad y Campo*, Lima, October-December, 1928.

Both Machu Picchu itself and the intihuatana,—the culminating feature of the prehistoric city,—are located and named on the map facing p. 348, in *Pérou et Bolivie*, by Charles Wiener, Paris, 1880.

[5] We use the word in the same sense,—as of "tying" a survey to some established base.

INTIHUATANA, MACHU PICCHU

Photograph by the author.

MASONRY OF PALACE WALLS, MACHU PICCHU

in strict accordance with the actual sun-year. It united
the social and religious life and ceremonies of the people
to their god, the sun. These sacred dials were always
erected at the highest point of the holy place, open to the
sky, in close proximity to the altar, sometimes, as at
Pisac, with the temple built around them.

The intihuatana of Machu Picchu stands upon the
furthest point of the city towards the great natural bar-
bican around which the turbulent river flows. Beyond
the sacred dial to the north the ridge narrows and breaks
down sharply, to rise again precipitately in the four-sided
pyramidal granite peak of Huayna Picchu. The stairways
and walled terraces upon the flattened top of the ridge
overhang the perpendicular walls of the chasm,—2,500
feet above the river. Next to the sun-dial on the crest of
the ridge is a small temple with several windows open to
the east and west. A curious feature of this building is
the stone ring projecting from its base, and forming a
part of one of the larger dressed stones composing the
wall. The stone is perfectly cut and fitted into the wall
and does not differ from the other large stones composing the base of the building except for this strong and
perfectly carved ring projecting from its outer surface.[6]
A great sacrificial rock stands by the shrine.

Towards the east, beyond the panorama of serried
ridges, the white peak of Chicón rises to a height of
nearly 20,000 feet. The shadows fall in the stupendous

[6] This remarkable stone ring was possibly intended for hitching the
sacrificial animal while awaiting the sacrifice. Of necessity planned before
the building was erected, this fastidious convenience illustrates the meticu-
lous forethought for the most trivial detail with which the ancient Peruvian
architects accomplished their results.

cañons,—a changing perspective,—while the morning sun
illumines the freshly fallen snows of the mighty peak,
and rises through the rose and golden clouds that hang
about its summit.   The river seems but a silver ribbon in
its labyrinthine gorge.   The sunlight falls here and there
in bright patches upon the ferns and orchids which find
precarious lodgment on the steep granite walls and illumines portions of the dense tropical forests crowding in the
detritus at the foot of the cliffs and on the alluvial slopes.
The shadows as they slowly descend into the cañons and
rise on the other side mark the progress and passage of the
day until the sun sets behind the empurpled snow peaks of
Panta and Soiroccocha,—two white islands floating in an
amethyst mist.   When dusk has fallen in the deep quebrada, a shaft of light beyond the ridges to the south still
glows upon the white crest of Salcontay as though it were
in the full brilliancy of noonday.

From the high rock on which the little temple stands a
splendidly constructed winding granite stairway leads
down along the crest of the ridge a short way towards
the south to two massive and palatial buildings occupying
two sides of a small open plaza.   They are merely one-
story walls of massive white granite blocks, some of which
in the lower parts of the walls are of huge size and all
perfectly cut and fitted.   In each building there are only
three walls, the front towards the plaza being left open,
—no doubt, when occupied, to be closed by curtains hung
on wooden curtain beams.

In one of these buildings there are three handsome
windows, of characteristic wedge-shape, opening to the

east and overlooking the steeply sloping city. A portion
of the gables, built of smaller stones, which supported
the roof of this structure, is still standing. At regular
intervals stone cylindrical projections on the outer side of
the gables, near the upper edge, suggest the idea of protruding roof-beams after the manner of the conventional
rudimentary stone beam ends in Greek architecture.
These gable knobs, however, were not merely ornamen-
tal, but were no doubt actually used for tying to them the
ends of the wooden roof beams.

The other palace consists of barely more than the three
walls, magnificent as they are,—though carved holes for
beam-ends in the front, stone benches, rows of handsome
niches with projecting knobs, for curtain poles, above
their interspaces, suggest the comfort and elegance with
which the royal house may have been furnished and
adorned,—with vessels of art and rich stuffs of vicuña and
alpaca.

Another stairway of white granite monolithic treads,
laid with such exactness that they are still in place and
serve perfectly the convenience for which they were intended, leads between the walls of a group of elegant
houses with steep gables and handsome doorways, with
great monolithic lintels, to the magnificent tomb of the
Inca,—a semicircular tower, rising high over an enormous
granite boulder to which, as a foundation, it is joined
with such solidity and perfection as to seem a part of it.
A small but handsome window opens out of the tower
towards the rising sun and the rock on which it is founded
rises within its walls as an altar and place of worship and

sacrifice. Underneath the rock is the cave of burial, handsomely walled in with cut stone, with various blind doorways of handsome proportions, or actual ones sealed in, which have not been opened. The outer vault itself has long since been broken into and rifled of any royal mummy it may have contained.

The tower and vault are flanked by a long temple wall of most exquisite workmanship with idol niches of the conventional size and shape,—some two feet two inches high and one foot four inches wide at the bottom, narrowing towards the top. Stone beam-ends project from the entablature of the niches, above the interspaces,—supports for rods for decorative or protective curtains. The stones of this wall are selected with the greatest care. Each is of the finest granite, without a flaw, perfectly cut and fitted, and so graded in size from the base to the top as to create a most pleasing impression. It is the masterpiece of the holy place of the city.

Adjoining these sanctuaries to the south is a great group of elaborate buildings, perhaps the convent of the nuns, or sacred virgins. It is entered through a handsome gateway supplied with bolts and locks fashioned in the lintels and jambs. These buildings are constructed of smaller and less finished stones of irregular size and alignment, but firmly built. Narrow corridors, like little alleys, run between them, and stone stairways ascend from one street level to another.

Small aqueducts, now dry, brought water to handsomely cut fountain basins, and led it from one to another through a series of fourteen such receptacles,— many of them cut in beautiful form, each from a single

ROYAL TOMB, MACHU PICCHU

Note in lower right corner the manner in which the natural rock is braced, and a bit of the beautiful mausoleum wall below. The burial vault is underneath the rock. The wall of the opposite side of the tower is curved.

Photograph by the author.

stone.[7] These fountain basins are shallow, of oblong rectangular shape, and show great taste in their design.

A long flight of granite steps leads down past the
fountains to the lower borders of the city and perhaps

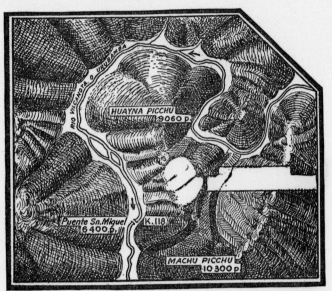

"Ciudad y Campo," Lima.

VERTICAL TOPOGRAPHICAL VIEW OF MACHU PICCHU

The city lies on the ridge between Machu Picchu (Big Peak) and
Huayna Picchu (Little Peak). At some points the precipice on which
the city is built falls perpendicularly for more than 2,000 feet into
the river cañon.

further down the steep eastern slope towards the river.
Below the windowed palace there is a pocket in the
mountain-side, with some level ground. This was the

[7] One of these ancient fountains did good service for our party as we
failed to find the spring and used the water which stood in the old pre-
Inca basin, probably from the last rains. After straining the green moss
out of it and boiling it for twenty minutes to kill any germ it might
contain, we enjoyed very much cocoa and "stew" cooked in it.

ancient plaza and gathering-place of the city. On its further, or eastern, side a handsome stone stairway leads to great groups of buildings, terraces, and gardens on the higher ground which enclosed the plaza on that side and completely walled it in with these elaborate structures. Though in complete seclusion, the occupants of these buildings could overlook from their ramparted heights the activities of the Forum and the market place.

A small family of Indians have crept back through the jungle and live in a hut they have built in the ancient plaza. Such of their meager living as nature does not afford, they make from the corn, beans, and potatoes they raise on a reclaimed bit of the old terraces. This is all that is left of life amid the altars and palaces where royalty trod.

XIII

PACHACAMAC

On the rough automobile road down the coast, south from Lima, one soon passes Pachacamac,—the new road winding through the vast extent of its adobe-brick ruins. The older temple of Pachacamac, on lower ground near the road, still plainly shows the lines of its secret chambers which once reeked with the stench of human sacrifice. The later temple of the sun crowns a height by the sea, and is reached by a series of terraces and inclined passageways through its massive walls. The red paint is still on the plaster sides of the corridors, and the great row of a dozen tall niches facing the sea on the very summit are still grimy and black with the smoke of the torches which centuries ago illuminated sacrificial rites or signaled to passengers upon the sea. What a spectacle, from the sea or from the neighboring islands, must have been this level row of high-flaming chambers on the summit of the great pyramid which crowned the sea-girt hill!

To the east the view extends in the interminable perspective of the mighty cañon of Lurin, opening into the far heart of the cordillera,—the peaks lifting themselves higher and higher, on either side, into apparently impossible and endless heights in the dim distance until they blend in indistinguishable shapes with the lines of clouds which hang in dense masses above the higher summits.

Though the mountains lacked somewhat, at the season

when we visited Pachacamac, the vividness of colors of the winter when the intense greens, brought out by the moisture on the middle slopes, make a vivid contrast with the brighter reds and yellows of the mountain soil and rocks,—still in the midst of summer the varying shades of ridge behind ridge in the rising panorama vie with the delicacy of the colors of the nearer foothills,—fading in soft lavender and the most velvety mauve and gray into the amethyst mist of the distant gorge.

The ruined city spread all about us,—long walls of sun-dried adobe blocks climbing hills, crossing valleys, rising again in long lines towards the mountains, enclosing quarters of the ancient town long since buried in the sifting sands. The walls of palaces and chiefs' houses and of a citadel crowd each other upon a hill near the road; and between this and the temple of the sun extends a vast valley of the dead. This is pitted in many places by the excavations of investigators and treasure seekers, and yet, for the greater part, the vast necropolis remains untouched. A broad esplanade leads from the cemetery up to the temple of the sun.

A great central street, intersected and paralleled by many narrower streets, extends through the city, walled in by the high sides of the principal houses. Here and there, banked against these walls, are vast heaps of refuse, the "kitchen-middens" of the ancient people,—throwing some light on their ideas of personal and civic cleanliness, as well as on their food, artifacts, and culture. Their food was evidently, in the main, plain and poor, as even under the walls of great houses were heaps of clamshells of a kind of shellfish now scarcely thought edible, and small cobs of a miniature corn (maize) scarcely larger than popcorn. Ashes, potsherds of curious shapes and decoration, cloths, still fairly well preserved in the rainless climate, constitute a large part of these heaps which have not been carefully excavated.[1]

At the foot of the citadel and about the larger houses, on level ground, are large rectangular spaces, once enclosed in walls now almost disappeared, where evidently the slaves and working classes lived, at night, after coming in from their work. The laboring masses of the communist rule were sheltered, no doubt, by flimsy lodges of reeds and grass which have long since disappeared; but the camp itself is full of evidences of their occupation. Generations of cooking over the same ground have built up a deep deposit of ashes; and buried in this are many evidences of the rude life of the working classes in this hierarchical and aristocratic socialistic state.

[1] There is a great opportunity here by a careful examination of these kitchen-middens to obtain much information on the intimate life of these ancient coast people.

XIV

"OCOMAL"

Yon farthest world that on the horizon looms,
What are its deathless fames but dying breath?
Each cosmos is an isle of nameless tombs,
Its life oblivious death.

J. Macmillan Brown, *The Riddle of the Pacific.*

When the Mayan people of Uxmal were driven from
their home in Yucatan by the more warlike Aztecs they
carried with them in their southern migration the name
of their ancestral capital as well as their tribal culture,
and ultimately planted both in Peru. Ocomal, the name
of the ancient Quichua village some twenty-five miles
southwest of Chachapoyas in a direct line, in the salubrious temperate zone of altitude of the Andes of northern
Peru,—in the great grass-covered limestone hills which
form the eastern watershed of the Marañon,—is but the
written form of the guttural pronunciation, as transcribed
by the Spanish explorers and geographers, of the Mayan
name written Uxmal by the northern chroniclers as they
heard it spoken in Yucatan.

"At Uxmal the buildings consist of five considerable
groups, viz.—the Casa del Adivino [or Temple of the
Magician], which is a step-pyramid 240 feet long by 160
feet wide and 80 feet high, crowned by a temple 75 feet
long by 12 feet wide; the Casa de Monjas, a striking

erection of four oblong buildings on an extensive terrace."[1]

The "Governor's Palace" at Uxmal is 320 feet long, 40 feet wide, and 25 feet high. "Immediately southwest of the Governor's Palace is a huge truncated pyramid 200 by 300 feet at the base and 60 to 70 feet high."[2]

There are evidences of Quichua-Mayan culture in the numerous prehistoric monuments about Ocomal and Leimebamba in the beautiful highlands along the Utcubamba,—the borderland of clear streams and cold springs between grass and forest; in the numerous limestone caves of this region where have been found many artifacts of clay, wood, and bronze, articles of domestic use, weapons of war, religious idols; in the great ruins at Tingo, Huancas, Macras, Jalca, Tambo Viejo, Levanto,[3] and the walled embankments of the river Utcubamba. This region was evidently the seat of a considerable population which expanded there, carried on its great work and developed its institutions for centuries.

Ocomal bears the name of the ancient capital of the ancestors of the race in the north; and at Malca, on the hacienda of Cuelap, at an altitude of 9,630 feet above the sea, on the summit of a sharp ridge near Ocomal, there is, almost intact, a colossal temple-tomb, which in its immense extent, its series of huge terraces, its material and mode of construction,—of dressed stones set in mortar,— is characteristic of the type of the ruins of Uxmal.

[1] Walter Lehmann, "Central America," *Encyclopædia Britannica*, 11th ed., V, 678.

[2] "Uxmal," *Encyc. Brit.*, 11th ed., XXVII, 828.

[3] The first site of the Spanish Colonial "City of the Frontier," afterwards removed to its present location a short distance to the north, and now called Chachapoyas.

The great structure lies between Tingo and Ocomal, on the high divide between the watershed of the Utcubamba and the headwaters of the Jumete and the Guaya. The Jumete flows a little north of west and empties into the Marañon; the Guaya flows to the west of north and empties into the lower Utcubamba; while the Utcubamba itself, after flowing for some distance to the north, passing a little to the west of Chachapoyas, turns to the northwest along the southern base of the Cordillera de Bougará and empties into the Marañon. There are rich valleys sunk deep in the high hills on all these streams, which in ancient times were well farmed and densely populated.

To the north and west the ridge on which the temple of Malca stands falls off more than fifteen hundred feet in nearly perpendicular precipices into the gorge of Celcas. The huge limestone cliffs on these sides meet at right angles. The central altar stands on the point of the angle of these precipices overlooking the abyss. The great structure, which is really a combined temple, mausoleum, and citadel, rises from the east by a series of two vast terraces supported by walls of dressed limestone blocks,— constituting in some respects the most gigantic structure on the American continent.

Towards the east the declivity slopes on a gradient of ten feet to the hundred. Along this slope from the edge of the precipice on the north the wall of the first terrace, —approximately half a mile in length and varying with the curvature of the ground from forty to sixty feet in height, of stones cut in regular angles to the slope of the wall and laid with great skill in even rows,—extends southward parallel with the line of the precipice on the

FORTALEZA DE CUELAP.

CASA EN JALCA
Detalles de Arquitectura.

Vista de una de las dos casas que aun conservan con esmero las autoridades del pueblo de la Jalca. Es indudable que son del tiempo incáico ó preincáico. Este dibujo fué hecho sobre un plano que levantó el Sr. Wertheman el año 1874, y que le mostró al Sr. Wiener.

Litografía, Abela. Lima.　　　　　　*Enrique Jiménez Glosgaro.*

—From article by Wertheman, cited.

(ABOVE) DETAIL OF THE RUINS OF EXTERIOR WALL OF CUELAP

The V shaped entrance is six feet wide at the outer end, narrowing to two feet at the inner end. It leads by a gently inclined way to the first terrace. This is the only opening in the outer wall. From the first terrace there are two such gateways leading by similar inclined ways through the second wall to the upper terrace.

The structure in the lower part of the picture is a *chulpa*, or tomb, still standing at Jalca, in the same neighborhood,—similar to those which stood on the great upper terrace at Cuelap.

west, and then turns in a rounded corner to a direction
at right angles with this, towards the abyss.

The face of this wall slopes slightly inward. The
space behind is filled in with earth to a level with the top
of the wall so as to form a platform or terrace. Upon
this platform stands another wall of similar construction, above and parallel to the first, and in its northern
part, for a space, superimposed upon the first wall. It
rises above the first terrace to a height of thirty feet,
forming, in that part where the two walls join, a slightly
sloping escarpment ninety feet in height, rising to the
level of the crest of the ridge. The exposed esplanade
of the first terrace, lying in front of the base of the
second wall, varies from one hundred and fifty to two
hundred and fifty feet in width. The wall of the second
terrace curves more or less parallel with the outer wall
and ends on the brink of the precipice lying along the
west side of the ridge.

The edge of the western precipice has been capped with
a level course of masonry and the space between it and
the second wall has been filled in with earth and loose
stone so as to form a second great platform extending half
a mile along the ridge level with the highest point of the
crest, from three to four hundred feet in width. A stone
parapet runs along the brink of the abyss.[4]

[4] The gateways in the walls are singularly like the entrance passage to
the final height of the great temple of Pachacamac. The general conception of the high-place of Pachacamac,—successive terraces of great
size,—greatly resembles that of Malca. However, Pachacamac, built of
adobe blocks, great as it is and magnificent as is its location,—the Pacific
beating at its base on one side and the perspective of the mighty gorge of
the Andes on the other,—does not approach the great stone temple of
Malca in the immensity of its structures nor in the superb grandeur of
its site.

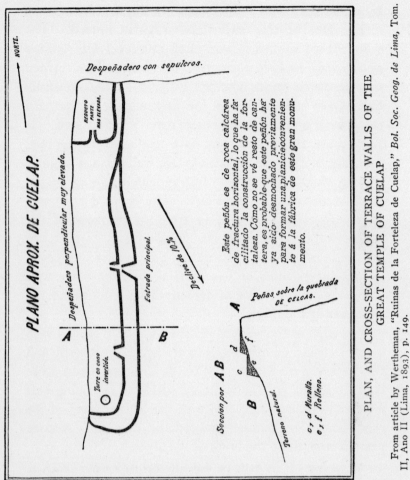

PLAN, AND CROSS-SECTION OF TERRACE WALLS OF THE
GREAT TEMPLE OF CUELAP

From article by Wertheman, "Ruinas de la Forteleza de Cuelap," *Bol. Soc. Geog. de Lima*, Tom. II, Ano II (Lima, 1893), p. 149.

Upon each side of the central part of this upper platform are the tombs of the ancient kings,—circular stone
structures similar to the burial *chulpas* about Lake Titicaca. Those on each side are united by a stone wall, each
series being thus formed into a single structure. In the
interior of the tombs are oblong idol or mummy niches
illuminated with a lining of white plaster. At the
extreme southern end of this terrace is a chulpa of special
design,—a truncated cone inverted,—of exquisite masonry,
twenty-three feet in diameter at the bottom and twenty-
nine and one half feet in diameter at the top.[5] It is encircled by a cornice thirty-one and one half inches wide,
of elaborate design. On this same second great platform
there are large cisterns, "which must have served to hold
rainwater, since there is no water on the hill except at a
great distance."

There are many burial niches in the face of the precipice which falls into the abyss on the northern side of the

[5] These figures and others are taken from an article by A. Wertheman,
Boletín de la Sociedad Geográfica de Lima, II, 148-153. He does not
give the height of this magnificent burial chulpa. "Among other objects,"
he says, "I will mention, besides the mummies and woven fabrics, a
large perforated bobbin of green quartz, a sling of cotton, and axes of
very hard bronze. . . . I sent to Dr. Raimondi three skulls. In one
there was a hole made by the blow of a stone, round as though made by
a bullet. We also found the skeleton of a man to which our attention was
especially called by its stature, and in order to convince myself I took the
femur to Dr. Raimondi, who calculated that it had belonged to an
individual about six feet five inches tall. The skull of this skeleton was
broken in pieces."

It may have been the skeleton of the Emperor, slain as he defended the
holy citadel.

On the general subject of these ruins, see Report of an expedition sent
out by the Prefect of the Department of Amazonas at the request of the
Lima Geographical Society, id., pp. 153-160; also Dr. Charles H. T.
Townsend, "South America Under the Equator," *Brazilian American
Magazine*, November 1, 1924 (Rio Janeiro).

altar,—sepulchers of lesser personages. These secure burial vaults hanging over the gorge were reached from the temple by precarious footholds cut in the face of the cliff and by ropes let down from above.

Superimposed on the second great terrace, above the brink of the precipices, on the very point of their north-west angle, rises the third and final level,—a walled platform of similar construction to the first two but more highly finished,—the altar of the "high-place,"—some forty-five feet square, retained in walls of polished stone. These walls incline slightly inward, and display the utmost perfection of workmanship. This altar is built around a natural rock, the culminating sharp apex of the peak, like those of Pisac and Ollantaytambo. The acute climax and finished expression of the mountain is thus made the center of the supreme altar,—the very heart of the high holy place. Surrounded and served by the magnificent artificial platforms,—its base the broadening foundations of the rocky ridge,—the very mountain itself is thus converted into a temple.

A V-shaped portal (narrowing from the front towards the interior), in the southern wall of the high altar, leads by an inclined way to its summit.[6] In the center of the

[6] Dr. Wertheman says: "For mounting to the top of this observatory [evidently referring to the high altar, the supreme culmination of the temple] there are two wings of dressed stone which enclose an inclined plane. . . . This granite has been brought from the banks of the Marañon, God knows by what roads, since no granite is found nearer. The entire hill and its surroundings are of limestone.

"All of the plinths of the doorways are of diorite, which undoubtedly has been brought from the eastern slope of the cordillera of Jalca, ten leagues from Cuelap. . . .

"There is no doubt that the whole Department of Amazonas was in-habited by a unique race which had ashy blonde hair, since all of the mummies taken from the tombs of Malca, Huancas, Tingo, etc., have

altar is a "bottle-shaped" octagonal well supplied with a square lid, or cover, made of a "beautiful polished diorite stone." The well is cut in the living rock which forms the center of the altar,—and was no doubt used in connection with the sacrificial ritual. It is twenty-two inches in diameter at the mouth and widens towards the bottom. It it partly filled in and its depth has not been explored.

Artistically sculptured in relief on red granite blocks set in the south wall of the altar, one on each side of the entrance, were the faces of a man and a woman supposed to represent the god and goddess of the sun and moon.[7]

blonde hair and no other kind. Many of the mummies have been taken to Europe on various occasions and there should have been published opinions on the subject of this race."

I have myself seen, in the great cemetery of Pachacamac and in the tombs among the wilderness of ruins between Lima and Callao, skulls still covered with reddish hair of fine texture, quite different from the coarse black hair of the modern Indian.

The terraces of the great temple of Malca are now covered with a growth of trees and bushes and even the walls themselves are partly obscured by grass and cactus.

Señor Wertheman says that near Tambo Viejo, also overlooking the great cañon of the Marañon (in the District of Ocomal), "a great pueblo, situated on a hill which commands the quebrada of Jinés, was discovered in our trip with Doctors Stübel and Reiss while we were looking for a strayed mule. This pagan village numbers eighty-four houses which can be made out today."

There are immense ruins of a great town near Molino Pampa, and quite extensive ruins of large stone buildings in a pleasant high valley above Leimebamba, on the trail to Balsas. There are many unexplored ruins in the agreeable, temperate, wooded, and well-watered country far east of Chachapoyas, beyond the high sierra of Pucaladrillo, about Punta Salas.

[7] A. Wertheman, *ibid.*

In the rather rambling and careless report of the Prefect's Committee, already referred to, it is said that these sculptures were placed one above the other. The report of this Committee also states: "The face of the woman sculptured in the lower stone shows a cap, much like those in use today, without a visor; and the regularity of the lines and features greatly differentiates this work from those which we know as of the time of the Incas."

The report states that the male figure has been destroyed in an effort to remove it.

The supreme altar commands a magnificent view of the deep valleys which radiate from the temple-crowned height. The great cordillera beyond the gorge of the Marañon, the wooded mountains of Jalca about Leimebamba and the headwaters of the Utcubamba, the high plateau of Chachapoyas, cut by deep cañons and merging into the summits of the central cordillera of the Andes, encircle the horizon in a mighty panorama.

This sacred center of prehistoric culture beyond the Marañon was only one hundred and forty miles in a direct line from the capital of the Grand Chimu and the Moche temples of Llampellec on the Pacific, and half that distance from the mountain highway of migration, later the road of the Incas, between Quito and Cuzco; but it was isolated and detached by a rugged range of mountains and by the profound cañon of the Marañon. The pleasant valleys were filled with an industrious and skillful agricultural people, who, though so near to the rich centers of population on the coast, developed behind their barricades of mountains and rivers a distinct and separate culture.

Like the Gothic cathedrals of medieval Europe, the enormous open temple of Malca is an expression of the religious devotion of a whole people. Like them no doubt it was long in building. Moved by the powerful sanction of their gods who controlled the seasons; commanded by kings who were themselves incarnate gods; conjured by priests who communed directly with the supreme powers of nature,—they gave themselves as a people to the erection of this mighty altar and royal tomb.[8] It stands on its princely heights as the supreme expression and record of a race.

As they looked up from their homes in the valleys or the far pastures on the hills, they found through it communion and immediate contact with their gods. The mummies of their ancestors preserved in the niches of the cliffs underneath the altar, the bones of their kings in the royal mausoleum on the terrace, enhanced the sanctity of the holy place. It was open to the glories of the sun, and the matchless beauties of the night in the clear mountain air where the goddesses of the moon and stars floated in unrivaled brilliancy in the heavens. No roof obstructed the sympathetic union of the people with the spirits of the sun and moon. The incense of the sacrifices rose directly to the heavens. On the supreme altar, high above the broad terrace, towering on the edge of the converging abysses, the column of smoke by day and of flame by night comforted the people as a "common supplication."

From the high-place the signal messages to the people far below directed their actions in harmony with the sun as he moved in the cycle of the year. In his daily passage over the heavens, wrapped in storm or enthroned in gold and silver, the high open temple was responsive to

---

[8] No doubt all contributed to the great work, as only in this way can the erection of such a colossal structure be explained. Men, women, and children probably shared when and as they were able in the work.

This was evidently the case in the building of the huge pyramidal altar-tombs which lie near the route of the Avenida Progreso, near Bellavista, at Lima. In the last-named structures adobe bricks of many shapes and sizes, apparently made by many different people, each after his own design and capacity, were skillfully worked by the masons into uniform structures: but little more, after all, from an architectural standpoint, than huge pyramidal heaps of bricks and earth, remarkable chiefly for their enormous size.

every mood of light and shadow. As he rose over the heights of Pishcohuañuna or sank behind the cordillera of the Marañon, the altar was often effulgent with his light while the abysses below were wrapped in twilight.

What a scene must have been here the ritual of the royal dead! The boom of the drums mingled with the shriek of the pipes in the wild barbaric music of the funeral march, as the long procession of priests in gold and scarlet robes mounted from terrace to terrace, bearing the decorated mummy to the imperial chulpa. On the high altar the blood of the sacred virgins, sacrificed to the dead, poured in a stream into the mystic well in the center of the sanctuary.

XV

THE SPREAD OF ABORIGINAL AMERICAN CULTURE

FIFTY-FIVE distinct languages are spoken by as many linguistic stocks of American Indians north of Mexico.[1] This excludes the still greater number of distinct dialects. Many writers in considering these and other differences seem to imply that these represent fifty-five distinct races coming from fifty-five separate and distinct origins. The tendency is almost universal to emphasize the differences and minimize the similarities.

All the artificial classifications of the human race into distinct divisions likewise underestimate the similarities to each other possessed by all branches of the human family; and many ignore completely the gradual merging of one race into another,—the constant effect of environment in modifying types of the same stock, the process of the fusion of the blood of all races in contact with each other having its varying effect throughout countless ages,—until it is impossible to say where one type leaves off and another begins. Every scheme of hard-and-fast classification is artificial, and leads to confusion and contradictions. In the true sense there is but one race of man, with innumerable variations.

In the old state of Virginia one can tell by a man's

[1] Franz Boas, Bureau of American Ethnology, Bulletin 40, Part 1, pp. 82-83.

accent what section of the state he comes from and in
some cases even from what county. In New York and
London there are people who have the peculiarities of
a certain street or alley which they have never left; and
in the coal mines of Northumberland County in England
there are said to be human beings born and grown to
maturity in the mines without ever seeing the light of day.
They have the language of the mines, the mine pallor,
the habit of the troglodyte.

But all this is the result of special chance and environment which creates an infinite variety of types in every
nation. The differences of races are but a wider opera-
tion of the same principle,—the effect of sun, or cloud, or
cold, or heat, of the nomad life upon the steppes of
Siberia, or of settled farming in the burning heat of
Africa, modifying, in innumerable special ways imper-
ceptibly merging into one another, the one great human
race, as it follows the sea or the land.

The inevitable tendency of language is towards divergence; and this is much more the case with the spoken
language than with the written. The Latin races of
Europe in modern times have developed in a comparatively short period by a process of evolution, assimilation,
and stress of environment, with infusions from many
other tongues, four great national languages [2] from the
original Latin, besides many subsidiary dialects. In parts
of France there are dialects unintelligible in other parts of
the country; and in China while there is one classic
written language and a single nation there are many

[2] Roumanian is perhaps a fifth.

vernaculars which are unintelligible outside their own localities.

It is but natural that the savage American Indian,— though mainly of one race and origin,—without a written language, engaged in a fierce struggle with nature under an enormous variety of circumstances and conditions, through many thousands of years, should have developed a diversity of languages. But the similarities of men in all parts of the world are more remarkable, more numerous, more interesting, and more fruitful study than their differences. And this is especially true, though so much neglected, of the indigenous American both North and South.

A distinguished specialist in Indian philology says:

"If, however, we want to follow a safe method, we must not admit such causes for sporadic distribution [of ethnic phenomena] unless they can be definitely proved by other evidence; otherwise the way is open to attempts to bring into contact practically every part of the world with all others." [3]

This illustrates the attitude of many specialists who reject the monistic theory of man's evolution and puzzle themselves and others over mysteries insoluble except on the acceptance of that obvious truth. Why bar the way of truth, as in the extract quoted, by excluding on an *a priori* basis, as a preliminary of a so-called scientific examination, the continuous contact and expansion of the human race throughout the world! How otherwise was the human race, which after all is but one race, dis-

[3] Franz Boas, Bureau of American Ethnology, Bulletin 40, Part 1, p. 52.

Stone piles made by Quichuas, each depositing a stone on crest of hill near Cuzco as they passed the summit on their journey. The Cherokees had the same custom. The practice was probably brought from Central Asia by the ancestors of the Quichuas and the Cherokees. It is followed by the Tibetans (*The World, Its Cities and Peoples*, Cassel and Company) at the present day.

The placing of a stone in the heap is by way of an offering of thanksgiving to God for having brought the traveler so far on his journey. It also implies a prayer for further protection.

tributed in every continent and in remote islands if there were no feasible passageway to all parts?

And when man himself traveled these routes, throughout the ages and in modern times, why assume that he did not carry with him into every part, in various eras, his language, arts, tools and weapons, religion and social organization;—changed, of course, specialized, modified by time, environment and experience; lost at times, fused with his friends or enemies and so passed on in new directions?

But the contact existed. The power of hereditary custom was persistent, as it is throughout the world today, and yielded only to the imperious necessity of new conditions, or to inventions whose benefit was so obvious as not to be resisted. But the play and interchange of old and new, the slow or swift influence that passed into "far countries" even in archaic times, left as sure proofs of world-wide continuity and transfusion of mental concepts and mode of life as of physical type. It can be traced in the gradual divergence of the most widely separated peoples.

Though the Alleghenies, interminable forests, and many hostile tribes intervened, the Catawbas disseminated in South Carolina their Siouan stock from the foothills of the Rockies. The great Cherokee race, though vast regions intervened between them and their northern brothers, spread throughout the great valley of Tennessee the blood of the Iroquois. Though no visible contact remained, this splendid family wielded its power on the banks of the St. Lawrence and the shores of the Gulf of Mexico.

Maize, which apparently does not exist in a wild state, is supposed to have been developed in the valley of Mexico at a remote age, and was a powerful factor in the attainment of the comparatively high degree of civilization of the Toltecs. It was carried from one tribe to another or accompanied them on their migrations until it reached the furthest limits of soil and climate suitable to its production and became, with the native potato, the staple food of the Quichuas under the empire of the Incas, as it was of the Algonkians on the confines of Canada.[4]

[4] It is not at all certain that maize was not brought from China in very remote times by the earliest voyagers across the Pacific. It is said to have been brought by Arabs into Spain in the thirteenth century. See important authorities cited in the article on "Maize" *Encyc. Brit.*, 11th ed. Commerce was carried on between China and Arabia in great ships long before the time of Marco Polo.

Quite recently it has been discovered that maize has been for ages the principal food of the people in the remote river gorges of western China and eastern Tibet ("Through the Great River Trenches of Asia," by Joseph F. Rock, *National Geographic Magazine*, August, 1926), where the customs and appearance of the people are much like those of the Peruvian Andes. These remote regions have seldom been visited by Europeans or Americans since the discovery of America by Columbus. It is significant that the word *mais* meant *grain* in China.

Chincha, a pre-historic settlement on the middle Peruvian coast, has the same name as the ancient Chinese port which the English called Chinchu.

"Garcilasso writes that the people of Chincha preserved the tradition that their ancestors had come from a far country." T. A. Joyce, *South American Archaeology*, p. 189, London, 1912.

The evolution of the primitive conception of God of the "Great White Race" as it radiated from its central Asian home was much the same in all directions. Being Westerners ourselves we have assumed, without any particular reason for such an assumption, that the "westward course of empire" was "the whole thing." There is no cause for astonishment in discovering that the Proto-Aryans, as well as the Proto-Mongolians, sent out colonies from the central Asiatic cradle-land to the east as well as to the west. On the contrary it would have been surprising if this were not so. It seems probable that the trek of the early sun-worshippers toward the sunrise was earlier than that to the west.

The "linguistic unity of the civilized Aztecs with the rude Utes and Shoshones of the north is one of the most interesting ethnological facts in primitive America."[5]

Illiamna, the Indians call the volcanic snow peak on Cook Inlet, Alaska; and Illimani[6] likewise is the indigenous name of the mighty glacier-covered mass in the *Cordillera Real* of Bolivia,—the same conception of the "home of the spirit" in the dread and inaccessible heights, represented by the same word in opposite ends of the hemisphere.

[5] A. F. Chamberlain, "Indians, North American," *Encyc. Brit.*, 11th ed., XIV, 471.

[6] The transposition of letters is a common occurrence.

XVI

SWARMS FROM THE MEXICAN HIVE

THE Mexican racial name *Nahua,* or *Anahuac,* appears in places as widely separated as southern Utah [1] and as the racial title of the ancient tribe of *Anahua* in the Peruvian highlands, also in *Ahuac,* populous Peruvian Quichua village in the Huancayo valley. It is also embodied in the name of the sacred ancestral hill of *Anahuarqui* at Cuzco. [2] The Central American racial appellations *Maya* and *Quiché* were also borne by Peruvian tribes, no doubt of kindred stock. [3]

The *Colhuas* of Central America [4] were driven south and their name was conspicuous as that of the great *Colla* or *Colhua* race who occupied the Titicaca basin. They gave their name,—*Colla-suyu,*—to the southern quarter of the four divisions of *Tehuanti-suyu,* the Inca empire.

The name *Cuzcatlan* (with its Aryan termination meaning land of *Cuzcat*) in Salvador, just west of the Gulf of *Fonseca,* [5] was of the same root as the Mexican *Tezcuco* in the north, and the even more famous *Cuzco,* capi-

[1] "Anahuac," *Encyc. Brit.,* 11th ed.
[2] Markham, *The Incas of Peru,* p. 131.
[3] *Quiché* still survives in central Peru as the name of an Indian village. As to the Peruvian tribe Mayu, see De Avila, *Rites and Laws of the Incas* (Hak. Soc.), p. 110.
[4] *Popol Vuh,* p. xxix.
[5] The name probably referred to the conical volcanic peaks of the locality. See map, *Popol Vuh,* p. cxxxi. "The richest and most flourishing of the states of the Nahua language," *id.,* p. cci. Cuzco is said to mean navel and in the Quiché picture writings a conical volcanic peak is represented by a conventional drawing of the navel. Abbé Brasseur de Bourbourg.

tal of the Ayar-Incas in the Peruvian highlands. The tribal name of the *Calchaquis* of the western *Chaco*, about the southeastern foothills of the Andes,—"city builders, influenced by Quichua culture," [6]—was no doubt from the same root as that of the probably kindred tribe of *Cakchikels* of Mayan stock in Central America.

The sacred Nahua name of *Tula*, modified to *Tola*, marked settlements of branches of that race in what is now Colombia,—one on the east coast of the Gulf of Darien, the other in the center of the country on the left bank of the Magdalena River.[7] From the latter point the advance was natural to the plain of Bogotá, and thence further south along the Andes.

Tonopah, the name of the Peruvian god who appeared on Lake Titicaca in the form of a white man,[8] was also known in Nevada and has survived there as the name of the important town of Tonopah in that state. The title of the *Michoacan* race, which gave its name to a state in Mexico, was carried as far north as the Great Lakes,—perhaps by the Toltec copper-miners, who left the record of their northern settlements in the name of what is now the state of Michigan.

Branches of the same tribal stock crossed the Gulf of Mexico and occupied the country to the north in what is now a part of Georgia, Florida, Alabama, Mississippi, and Louisiana,—marked on the map of the distribution of Indian races as *Mushocean*.[9] The god *Saco* of the Darien

---

[6] *Johnson's Universal Cyclopædia*, IV, 553.

[7] Map, *Popol Vuh: Le Livre Sacré*, p. ccxxi.

[8] Salcamayhua, *Rites, etc., of the Incas* (Hak. Soc.), p. 71.

[9] J. W. Powell, "Map of Linguistic Stocks of American Indians North of Mexico," *Johnson's Universal Cyclopædia*, IV, 554. The word is spelled

Indians "appears identical with the *Saki* of *Hunsa*, in Bogotá." [10] As a record of a wider movement, *Tucume*, the name of an Indian village in Peru, reappears in the ancient title of what is now the province and city of Tucumán in the Argentine. The root of the word *Yakutat*, an ancient Indian village on the Alaskan coast, now well known as the site of a salmon cannery, is identical with that of the famous Yucatan (formerly spelled *Yukutan*) on the Gulf of Mexico and Caribbean Sea.

Quito, a place-name in Mexico, was brought to *Quito* in Ecuador in archaic times. *Chiriqui*, the tribal appellation of a fine tribe of Indians,—now farmers and herdsmen in the delightful mountain province of the same name on the Isthmus of Panama,—seems to have been carried in more primitive times across the Gulf of Mexico in a forced or voluntary migration in the great dispersion of tribes. At any rate, whatever the connection may have been, it was the family cognomen of the founders of the great *Cherokee* tribe who, at the time of the arrival of the Europeans, occupied a similarly beautiful hill country of woods and pleasant waters in and about the southern Appalachians.

With increased population on the plain of *Anahuac* and the reports of rich lands to the south and north, there

in many ways by the early chroniclers in their varied efforts to transmit to writing the sound of the word as it was spoken to them in the guttural Indian language. All of these forms of the word were closely related in the actual native pronunciation to the word *Mexican* itself. In transcribing the Central American and Mexican speech the Spanish writers used the letter *x* to express the equivalent of "the French *ch* or the English *sh*" (Brasseur de Bourbourg, *La Lengua Quiché*, p. 3), so that *Mexican* would be, in our letters, *Meshican*.

[10] W. Bollaert, *Antiquities, etc., of South America* (London, 1860), p. 26.

AGUARUNA INDIAN. UPPER MARAÑON RIVER, NEAR CHA-
CHAPOYAS, PERU

This man is probably of Carib stock. Note his light color and powerful
physique.

was a period of swarming colonies from the racial hive. This movement was accelerated by the constant bitter war to the death between the tribes, in which, as in Peru, the land was stubbornly fought for inch by inch and from one strategic fortress or vantage point to another.

The bloodthirsty religion of the Aztecs and other Mexican tribes, with its insatiable demand for sacrificial victims, furnished a constant motive for war.   In addition to invasion and conquest, hurricanes, inundations, great forest fires, and volcanic eruptions,—such as those occurring in our time at Galveston, Miami, Havana, and the Island of Martinique,—were among the causes of destruction or migration of races mentioned in the Nahua and Toltec traditions.[11]

As the Nahuas moved from one stage to another along the Pacific coast of the Isthmus, the Caribs,—described as a fierce and dominant race of powerful stature, with a strong strain of Caucasian blood,[12]—established their colonies along the Atlantic coast as far as Brazil, explored the Orinoco in their great canoes and carried their culture far into the interior.[13]   It is curious to note that the root, *Cari*, of their name, which appears in innumerable place-names in the vast domain covered by their migrations, was the name of a mythical chief of the legendary white race which settled on the shores and islands of Lake Titicaca,[14]—and was also the name of several of the later

[11] *Popol Vuh*, p. ccvi.
[12] *Popol Vuh*, p. ccxii.
[13] *Popol Vuh*, pp. cciii *et seq.*, ccvi.
[14] See the Polynesian legend of *Ari* (also called *Kari, Karii, Karihi*), S. Percy Smith, *Polyn. Jour.*, VIII, 1.   Both *Ari* and *Kari* were well-known family names in Scandinavia—no doubt brought there by the Aryans in early migrations from the east; e.g., "the Haurda-Kari family so famous

Ayar kings of Peru. This is said to be an Asiatic word meaning in general strong, handsome, excellent.[15]

A few years before the voyage of Columbus, a colony of the Caribs from the Mexican racial center had settled in the Antilles. "They felt themselves endowed with the personal qualities which seemed nearly always to be characteristic of the conquering races. . . . So they assumed the leadership of the neighboring people and arrogantly claimed that they alone were men and the others only slaves."[16] To those who are thoroughly familiar with the recent history of other branches of the Caucasian race, in all parts of the world, this characteristic kindred attitude seems strikingly familiar.

In these great folk-stirrings along the converging shores of the continent, nations of different customs and religion, many of them mutual enemies, were thrown in unavoidable contact on the narrowing Isthmus. Mixtures of varying cultures resulted. This fact will serve to explain many apparent racial anomalies.[17] The indigenous race of South America from the Orinoco to the Amazon and thence to the Plate was of yellow, Mongolian strain,

in the Orkneys" (Frederick York Powell, "Iceland, History and Ancient Literature," *Encyc. Brit.*); also the celebrated Icelandic writer *Ari* Thorgilsson, 1067-1148—"one of the blood of Queen Aud." *Ibid.*

The original significance of this root and its relationship, if any, to Ârya (Sanskrit, *Noble*)—to the Polynesian *Ari-ki* ("the chief descendant of the chief ancestor")—its ultimate root origin as it appears in *aristocracy*, its use in innumerable Greek proper names, such as *Aristotle*, afford an interesting speculation. Its Greek derived meaning, *good* (aristos, *best*), is probably related to its archaic Asiatic sense of *excellent*, even *divine*, as *Pa-ccari*, ancestor of the Ayars, *Ara* of the Colhuas. *Infra*, pp. 154, 167. *Ante*, pp. 28, 29, notes. Cf. "*Ari*, which is explained as 'active, devoted, pious.'" Peter Giles, "Aryan," *Encyc. Brit.*, 11th ed., II, 712.

[15] *Popol Vuh*, p. ccix, note.
[16] *Popol Vuh*, p. ccix.
[17] *Popol Vuh*, p. ccviii.

quite different from the Caribs, who were largely of Caucasian origin. The two peoples amalgamated and the tribes of Mongolian stock adopted the habits and mode of life of the Caribs. The Brazilian manner of wearing clothing, keeping fire by their beds, smoking the calumet of peace, showed their northern origin. The arrangement of their houses was like that of the Iroquois and Hurons.[18]

Objects of gold worked with a high degree of art, found in mounds in the province of Chiriquí, Panama, are attributed to a branch of the Carib race. In the forests of Veragua "imposing remains of an ancient civilization, tombs, palaces, colossal columns covered with fantastic sculptures, but which have nothing in common with the noble ruins of Palenque and Yucatan," mark the establishment there of a culture which at the time of the arrival of the Spaniards "was decayed if not extinct." [19] These remains of ancient art are ascribed to the worshippers of the *Ara (Ayar?) Vukub-Cakix*, a legendary leader who claimed to be the equal of the Sun and Moon.

[18] *Popol Vuh*, pp. ccxii, ccxiii. The Indians of the Brazilian *Matto Grosso* to this day call white men *Caraibas* (Caribs). "The Search for Colonel Fawcett," by G. M. Dyott, *Geographical Journal* (December, 1929), LXXIV, 526, 531, 532, 534, 538. The Wicurus in this region have "very light skins." *Id.*, p. 535.

[19] *Popol Vuh*, pp. cciii, cciv.

XVII

FROM *TEXCOCO* TO *TITICACA*, AND FROM *TEZCUCO* TO *CUZCO*

THE people who left the curious ruins of *Teotihuacan* on the shores of Lake *Texcoco* in the valley of Mexico, perhaps driven from this seat of their culture, after migrations of unknown duration planted these names in new homes where now stand the equally remarkable monuments of *Tiahuanaco* on the shores of the greater Lake *Titicaca* on the summit of the Andean plain.[1]

As the European ancestors of white colonists in both North and South America consoled themselves in the New World by fixing upon their pioneer settlements the hallowed and familiar names of ancestral villages in England

---

[1] " 'Cuzco, in the language of the Incas,' says Garcilasso (*Com. Real.*, Parte I, Lib. I, Cap. 18), 'signifies navel.' " Prescott, *Conquest of Peru*, I, 8, n. 7. This was from its central position in the Empire, both geographically and in the life of the people. The four highways from the four quarters of the realm, north, south, east, and west, crossed there at right angles.

Likewise Tezcuco—evidently the same word with the definite article prefix and the metathesis common in dialectical changes—*Te* (the)—*Cuzco*—occupied a similar central position on the borders of its lake in the high Mexican valley, the seat of royal and religious authority, with the four roads to the four cardinal divisions of the Kingdom crossing in the center of its plaza. (Tylor and Lehmann, "Mexico, Ancient Civilization," *Encyc. Brit.*, 11th ed., XVIII, 333.

Tiahuanaco (*Tia*, god; *huanaco*, from the Quichua *huaco*, idol or shrine; and *na*, place) was the holy place or shrine of the divinity. Teotihuacan, on the Mexican lake, with its pyramid temples, was likewise *Teoti*, god's, *huacan*, place of the shrine or temple (from *huaca*, temple; *an*, or *ana*, place). "It cannot be doubted that it (Tiahuanaco) is an ancient religious center of great importance, founded by the Toltecs." Raoul d'Harcourt, *L'Amerique Avant Colomb* (Paris, 1925), p. 90.

or Spain, the Teotihuaqueñans of the Mexican plateau carried the name of their city of Tezcuco and of Lake Texcoco, around which their civilization had developed in its mountain valley, to the southern extension of that same valley on the Peruvian and Bolivian plateau. There they gave it to the great and beautiful lake (now spelled, in the reduction of a spoken language to an alien writing through many hands, *Titicaca*) on whose shores they built their new homes.

There they left, when again conquered and driven out from their home, the remarkable and imperishable ruins of their temple.[2] Along with the name they brought maize; and there they placed the conception of their gods in the durable records of the grotesque stone figures of Tiahuanaco.

Cuzco (spelled *Cusca, Cosco, Cusco,* or *Cuzco,* as it sounded to various ears),[3] the famed capital of the Incas, perpetuates the name of Tezcuco, center of pre-Aztec culture in the valley of Mexico.

"The principal palace of Mexico consisted of hundreds of rooms ranged round three open squares, of such extent that one of the companions of Cortes records having four times wandered about till he was tired, without seeing the whole. Not less remarkable was the palace of Tezcuco, surrounded with its groves and pleasure-gardens; and, though now hardly anything remains of the buildings above ground, the neighboring hill of Tezcotzinco still has its stone steps and terraces; and the immense embank-

[2] Erected no doubt under white Aryan leaders from Polynesia, who had left similar memorials on Easter Island and in the Carolines.

[3] Juan Durand, *Boletín de la Sociedad Geográfica de Lima,* XXXII (1916), 1st quarter, p. 102.

ment carrying the aqueduct-channel of hewn stone which supplied water to basins cut in the solid rock still remains to prove that the chroniclers' descriptions, if highly coloured, were at any rate genuine." [4]

Very probably the name was carried to South America and the settlement made in the lovely valley of the Vilcanota in the cool highlands of the Cordilleran pampa, so much like their ancestral home in the north, by the descendants of the highly civilized Acolhuas, who were driven from Tezcuco by the ruder and bloodthirsty Aztecs.[5]

The merger, transposition, or elimination of letters or syllables through stress of climate or occupation upon the organs of pronunciation, and the universal tendency towards variation as words are carried in migrations, borrowed by one tribe from another, or as families divide into various branches, are illustrated in every language. Any book on genealogy shows the innumerable variations of family names. Saint Botolph's Town becomes Boston; *Rimac*, through the indisposition or inability of the coast natives, like the Chinese, to pronounce the letter "r," and the slurring of the letters, becomes *Lima*.

The Quichés of Guatemala, who had mastered the art of masonry, carried their civilization to the south and developed a local culture on the present site of Quito. Sometimes called Quitus,—as one of the various spellings by which European adventurers, explorers, and priests in-

[4] E. B. Tylor and Walter Lehmann, "Mexico: Ancient Civilization," *Encyc. Brit.*, 11th ed., XVIII, 332.

[5] In the time of the Incas, and before, this Mexican tribal name was preserved in Peru (spelled Colhua, Colla, etc., by various Spanish chroniclers). It designated the region of Lake Titicaca and its inhabitants,—*Colla-suyu*, the southern division of the Inca Empire.

PREHISTORIC QUADRANGLE OF MONOLITHS, TIAHUANACO

Photograph by the author.

A Cholo maiden of Cuzco. "An arresting and graceful piece of work, depicting the traditional and picturesque type of young womanhood so prevalent in La Paz and in the Bolivian-Peruvian highland, in general."

Yupanqui, a perfect example, of the warlike type of Amerindian. "In this study the sculptor has portrayed the highest types of Amerindian manhood. The broad full forehead, wide nostrils, full lips and firm mouth, the muscular neck, and the proud poise of the head mark the man born to direct, lead and rule. Yupanqui is, in short, an admirable example of the combative genius of the great warrior chiefs who, centuries ago, ruled the ancient and powerful civilisations of the Andean highlands."

Sculptures by the Spanish sculptor, Ramon Mateu. From "Bulletin of Pan-American Union," December, 1927.

terpreted in European letters the gutturals of the Indians,
—they became a part of the empire of the Andes under
the rule of the Incas.

The great southern branch of their family, the Quichuas, forms the bulk of the population of Peru today, as
it did of the Inca realm.   Further north, on the same
salubrious plateau of the continental chain on which both
Cuzco and Quito are located, the Chibchas (sounding in
Indian speech much like Quichuas) in the great valley
of Colombia, where the Spaniards founded the city of
Bogotá, developed a branch of Mayan culture.   On the
southern shores of Lake Titicaca, extending far into Bolivia along the Andean plateau, the Mayan stock, calling
themselves Aymarás, were settled at an early date, and
in turn, in the constant and innumerable tribal wars, became subject to the Quichua power under the Incas.

The peninsula of Nicoya extends in a southeasterly
direction from the northwest coast of Costa Rica.   The
tenth degree of north latitude crosses near the middle of
it.   Ruins of Mexican works similar to those found in
Guatemala, Salvador and Nicaragua have been discovered
in this peninsula.[6]   Kindred civilizations left their records
further east and south, and exploration of the isthmus
may disclose still further vestiges of the Mayan people.
However, from the most southern of the ancient settlements of the Mexican people so far discovered, on the
peninsula of Nicoya, a voyage of six hundred miles over
water free from storms and abounding in food, along a
coast affording abundant harbors, would have brought
them to the coast of the southern continent.

[6] Walter Lehmann.

Some fifty miles northwest of the modern city of Guatemala, along the foothills of the cordillera, at Santa Cruz del Quiché, on the table-land of Guatemala, stand today the extensive ruins of the Maya city of Quiché. Crowded from their homes by the fierce races of the north, branches of the same people, blended with others and modified by their surroundings, established their culture in the southern continuation of the same salubrious alto-plane, where their descendants, among the obscure memorials and monuments of their ancient civilization, can be traced in the miserable remnants of the Chibchas of Colombia, the Quitus of the Ecuadorian valley,—where was established one of the twin capitals of Huayna Capac,— the Quichuas of the highlands of Peru, and the Aymarás extending far south on the Bolivian table-land.[7]

"The war-god Huitzilopochtli was the real head of the Aztec pantheon; his idol remains in Mexico, a huge block of basalt on which is sculptured on the one side his hideous personage, adorned with the humming-bird feathers on the left hand which signify his name, while the not less frightful war-goddess Teoyaomiqui, or 'divine war-death,' occupies the other side."[8]

From this and other memorials of Mexican art and Mexican religion, the same influence and contact can be traced through the Maya ruins and is evident again in the stone of Chavin, discovered in 1840 by Timota Espinosa in the hamlet of Chavin de Huantar, on the Andean pla-

[7] "Scattering remains have been discovered all along, however, connecting the art of Costa Rica with that of Veragua, Panama, and the South American Continent." William H. Holmes, in *Report of U.S. Bureau of Ethnology, 1884-85*, pp. 13-14.

[8] Tylor and Lehmann, *supra*, p. 333.

"CHAVIN STONE," LIMA

Photograph by Harriett E. Meek.

teau, in northwestern Peru, and now preserved in the
National Museum at Lima.   It is a handsomely cut diorite
slab 6 feet 4.77 inches in length, 28.74 inches in width at
the top, 29.13 inches at the middle, and 29.92 inches wide
at the bottom.   It is 6.69 inches thick and the low-relief
carving on its face is .19 inch in thickness.[9]

On it are carved, with consummate art, the monstrous
features of the war-god of the Quichuas,—terrible fangs
of the "Devourer" protruding from his mouth, a three-
tiered "beast-mask" upon his head, serpents issuing from
various parts of his body.   He holds upright in each hand
a great symbolic scepter of authority.   Horns (of power)
issue from his forehead.   Serpents stream from his huge
head-dress.   Condors' heads appear with sinister expression, awful horned monsters leer and seem to grind and
clamp together in fury and lust of destruction their inter-
locking tushes, protruding like pointed sabers from their
hideous mouths.

Quiché, the name of the prehistoric city whose ruins
cover an extensive area of the highlands of Guatemala, is
reproduced in Peru in the important Indian pueblo of
Quichés, still inhabited by the descendants of the old race,
—on the western slopes overlooking the Marañon in the
province of Pomabamba.   Yucatán has been transplanted
to Peru in a modified form in Yaután, ancient Indian village on the Casma River in the province of Santa.

The fabled land of *Llampallan* to which *Quetzalcoatl*
sailed, in the Toltec legend, seems but *Llampallec* (now
the Peruvian province of Lambayeque), the Peruvian

[9] Reduced from metric measurements given by José Toribio Polo in *Bo-
letin de la Sociedad Geográfica de Lima*.   See illustration, Vol. II, p. 47.

domain of the Grand Chimu. Chimu legend supplemented that of Anahuac in telling of the arrival of the great leader and his royal suite. The name was carried into the high Peruvian Andes and still survives in the populous town of Ticlapallan between Huanuco and Cerro de Pasco.[10]

[10] The place-names Casmal, Tutumal, Cochamal, in the province of Chachapoyas, Peru, are quite suggestive of Mayan and Quiché nomenclature.

XVIII

COLONIZATION, TRADE, AND COMMUNICATION

COMAGRE, the Carib king of Darien, kept the embalmed mummies of his ancestors in a hall in his house [1] as was the custom of the Peruvians both in the cordilleras and on the coast.[2] "All this race of men so terrible and so cruel had issued from regions of Mexico to people Panama and Darien and the immense countries as far as New Granada and Santa Marta." [3]

In the north the mounds of the Mississippi Valley, with their remains of tall Caucasian men, were monuments of Nahua culture of the same general type as many of those built along the coast of Peru by other branches of the same race cast out of the Mexican matrix in the great tribal upheaval, and driven north and south in remorseless war from one colonization to another.[4] Some of these structures were altars,—others burial mounds of the same character as those in Asia, whose form and mode of

---

[1] *Popol Vuh,* p. cciv.

[2] Contact of Egyptian and Polynesian cultures (whether by the origin of the Polynesian culture in the Egyptian, either through direct descent or through mere "borrowing," or imitation, or by widely separated descent, possibly in opposite directions, of both from a common origin, otherwise the one not in any way connected with the other) is claimed by Dr. G. Elliot Smith to be indicated by the practice of mummification. "Significance of Geographic Distribution of the Practice of Mummification," *Manchester Memoirs,* LIX, 10, reviewed by H. D. Skinner, *Polyn. Soc. Jour.,* XXVI, 122.

[3] *Popol Vuh,* p. ccvi, citing Blas Valera.

[4] *Popol Vuh,* p. clxxii.

construction have changed little from primitive times to
the present day. A similar earthen mound is now being
heaped up over the grave of the late Japanese Emperor,
Yoshihito.

Driven from the interior to the Pacific Coast where
they built the city of *Tlapallantzinco*,—named after "the
sacred land of Tlapallan from which they had been
exiled,"—the Nahuas, fighting desperately for their pos-
sessions, were conquered and forced out again. They
migrated still further south.[5] "This great migration of
which the memory recurs so often in *The Sacred Book*
(*Popol Vuh*) and which the people sadly recalled in their
songs, was the same as that of the Toltecs of which Ixtlil-
xochitl gives the itinerary with the aid of maps left by
his ancestors in the archives of Anahuac."

Some family groups fled to the northwest and carried
elements of the Toltec culture,—the ritual of the worship
of the sun, belief in the immortality of the soul,[6]—into
northern Mexico and what is now New Mexico, Arizona,
and California.[7] The Sacred Book speaks of three great
dispersions of races from the Mexican and Central American focus. Some followed the coast and others went
directly across the sea,—no doubt to the north and east
across the Gulf of Mexico and the Caribbean, and to the
south across the great Colombian bight.[8]

The Central American traditions of the southward mi-

---

[5] *Popol Vuh*, pp. clviii, clix.

[6] *Popol Vuh*, p. clxxxviii.

[7] *Popol Vuh*, pp. clix, clx. The ceremonial sun-dance is religiously observed to this day by the northern Indians. Their orators invariably in-
voke the sun-god.

[8] *Popol Vuh*, p. clxv.

grations of the various branches of the Nahua peoples are corroborated by Peruvian legends of the arrival of immigrants in that country. Montesinos tells of "great bands of people" who "entered the Andes by way of Panama" in the reign of *Tocco-Cozque.* "They arrived at Cuzco and other villages of these provinces and settled down in them." Some came by the port called, by the Spaniards, Buenaventura, on the Colombian coast.[9] Montesinos undertakes to fix this immigration in the reign of *Tocco* [10] *Cozque,* eighty-second king in his genealogy of kings and before the advent of Ayar Manco,—but of course this is merely conjectural; and there were, no doubt, settlements on the coast of Peru of immigrants from the north for centuries before they penetrated inland to Cuzco, beyond the two principal cordilleras, in the far southeast.

This general tradition no doubt refers to many migrations from Panama, and further north, which arrived in Peru at various epochs, some of them in archaic times. "A very ancient tradition of the Indians says that from the district of the Audience of Quito, from the south bank and the north bank of the Marañon, came at several times great troops of people, as well by land as by sea, and they settled the coasts of the ocean and went inland by way of *Tierra Firme* (*sic*) so that they filled up these extensive kingdoms which we call Pirú." [11]

[9] *Memorias Antiguas* (Hak. Soc.), p. 66.

[10] Note the practical identity of this name with the Japanese *Togo.*

[11] *Memorias Antiguas,* p. 14. An Indian tradition combining a plausible account of early racial migrations from the north with obviously mythical embellishments is repeated by the Jesuit padre, Anello Oliva. This chronicler completed his work, *History of Peru and the Company of Jesus,* in 1631. "The first people came to South America from parts unknown, landing somewhere on the coast of Venezuela. From there they gradually

The tradition to which this brief reference is made must have been a basic and familiar legend to the Peruvians. The pressure from north to south to which it refers was undoubtedly caused by attacks made on the tribes of the Marañon, in the temperate mountain country about Chachapoyas and Cajamarca, by invaders from further north, —and the process described had no doubt been going on from the most primitive times.

Brasseur de Bourbourg recalls that the Icelandic Sagas referred to the Atlantic coast of what are now Georgia and the Carolinas as *Great Ireland* and also as *White Man's Land*. The Sagas relate that *Ari* (*Ayar* or *Aryar?*) was thrown ashore there by a tempest and settled in the country. Even as late as the sixteenth century the Spaniards,

scattered over the whole continent, one band reaching the coast of Ecuador near Santa Elena. Several generations passed, many made voyages along the coast and some were shipwrecked. At last one branch took up its abode on an island called Guayau near the shores of Ecuador. On that island Manco Capac was born and after the death of his father Atau he resolved to leave his native place for a more favored clime. So he set out in such craft as he had with two hundred of his people, dividing them into three bands. Two of these were never heard from again but he and his followers landed near Ica on the Peruvian coast, thence struggled up the mountains, reaching at last the shore of Lake Titicaca." (Adolph F. Bandelier, *The Islands of Titicaca and Koati*, p. 325.)

As the legend proceeds, features of both the *Titicaca* and the *Paccari Tampu* myths appear in it. Bandelier says, "Its reliability is doubtful," and gives in much detail reasons for his conclusion. No doubt much of the relation is not only "doubtful" but obviously incredible. Nevertheless the central feature of the tradition (which Oliva says he obtained from an old Indian *quipu-camayoc*, one skilled in keeping and interpreting the records kept on the *quipus*, or knotted cords)—of migrations from the north which came by way of Venezuela, spread to the coast of Ecuador and after generations there came further south in search of a better climate,—is corroborated not only by other chroniclers and by much tangible archæological proof but by the strong probabilities of the case. This is by no means all of the story,—as there were many migrations by different peoples in various widely separated epochs,—but there is a verisimilitude in the moving incidents of the old Indian's tale of the great racial adventure which is convincing.

"bent on gold and conquest," found there nations of warriors of remarkable size and strength.[12]

One of the settlements on the right bank of the Mississippi was recognized as of undoubted Nahua origin by its name,—*Tula*. In the country north of the Gulf of Mexico the tribes had developed a high degree of culture and progress. There was a great confederation with a king who ruled over an extensive territory and was the lord of many subordinate chiefs. His domain extended to the Antilles. These immigrants retained many features of Mexican civilization. They had strongly fortified strongholds, houses enclosed in high walls, roads, canals, fish ponds, enclosed fields; and it is asserted by many chroniclers, including de Soto, that they had domesticated the deer and made cheese from its milk.[13]

The Nahuas searched for a terrestrial paradise,—to which they gave the name of *Tamoanchan*,[14] marked on the map published by Bourbourg as what is now the southwest coast of Yucatan, fronting on the Gulf of Mexico.[15] This name is reflected in that of the Indian people and their language and town on the left bank of the Mississippi at its mouth,—*Hitimachan*,—and in *Timuouanan*, covering Florida, scene of Ponce de Leon's search for the terrestrial paradise.[16]

An active commerce was carried on throughout the Caribbean and the coasts of the mainland, and the leaders

---

[12] *Popol Vuh*, p. clxv.

[13] *Popol Vuh*, p. clxvi. The mere existence of this report is surprising. The animal referred to may possibly have been the elk or the bison.

[14] *Popol Vuh*, p. lxxviii.

[15] *Popol Vuh*, p. cxxxi.

[16] J. W. Powell's Map of Indian Tongues, *Johnson's Universal Cyclopædia*, IV, 544.

and wise men had an extensive knowledge of the people
and the geography of a great part of the two continents.[17]
Communication had existed with Peru from ancient times.
"The first news which Balboa had of Peru, as well as of
the Pacific, was given to him by a young chief of Comagre
who, pointing to the south, said to him: 'In that direction
you will find princes who use only vessels of gold. Navi-
gation there is carried on in ships with sails and oars,—
almost as large as your own.' A little later it was the
Chief of Tumaco who traced out for Balboa, on his arrival in the Bay of Panama, the outline of the coasts of
Quito,—describing to him at the same time the riches of
gold of Peru and the strange shape of the llamas *which
carried ores in the cordillera,*—which the Spaniards took
to mean camels." [18]

Brasseur de Bourbourg makes the sagacious remark that,
considering it was many hundreds of leagues from the
Isthmus to the country of which the cacique had such exact
knowledge, there are very few among us today, or among

[17] There are many traces in the words and metaphors of the common
speech of these people not only of contact with each other, but of broader
relationships with the archaic sources of the Indo-European tongues. Cf.
Mayan *tip*, point, or extremity; English, *tip* (Bourbourg, *Langue de Mayas*,
II, p. 373). Nahuatl, *paca*, woolly; Quichua, *alpaca* (T. S. Denison, *Mex.
Ling*, p. 86). Nahuatl, *atl*, water; Atlantic, composed of *atl*, water, *an*,
place, *tic*, adjectival ending.
Peruvian, *mama*, mother; Mexican, *papa*, father. The same general
sense of both words obtained with the Greeks, Romans, and other Indo-
Europeans. In Mexico *papa* was a priest of high rank, the same as our
Pope. Prescott, *Conq. Peru*, I, 9, n. 8. With the Peruvians *mama* was also
the name of the sea, the same as the French *mer*, sea, (*mère*, mother), the
Spanish *mar* (from L. *măre*, sea; *măter*, mother; Spanish, *madre*, mother).
The root from which all these words are derived probably had the sense
of *source, origin*. Cf. Polynesian *meremere*. Curiously the Spanish have
masculinized the mother sea and call it *el mar*.
[18] *Popol Vuh*, p. ccvii. Italics mine. M. P.

the Spanish-Americans, even in the educated classes, who are so well-informed.[19]

Throughout the vast region of these settlements trade was actively carried on, very largely by the easy and innumerable waterways of the rivers and along the coast. As in Asia, commercial fairs were held at stated times in all of the principal towns, "to which merchants resorted from a distance of many hundreds of miles by sea and land."[20] Indian corn,[21]—a native plant of Mexico, and the basic food supply of the Mexicans and Central Americans,—had been carried in remote ages to Peru, where it underwent much special development.

Though agriculture had been developed in Peru to a much higher degree than in Mexico or Central America, there were many points of similarity in the agricultural methods of the northern and southern peoples, not only as to the cultivation, but as to the control and distribution of the soil. Both north and south, subject to the eminent domain of the king, "the arable land was chiefly in the possession of the villages, and was let out to individual cultivators under careful regulation."[22]

Turquoise was brought, partly by land and partly by water, to Yucatan from as far north as the present New

[19] *Popol Vuh*, p. ccix.

[20] D. G. Brinton, "Indians of Central America," *Johnson's Universal Cyclopædia*, VI, (1900), 207.

[21] Said to be derived from the Mexican and Central American plant, *Euchlæna luxurians* (D. G. Brinton). As this remarkable grain has apparently for centuries been the principal food supply of tribes in the river gorges of western China and about the borders of Tibet, only recently visited by Europeans, doubt has been expressed of its origin in America. By others it is said to have been imported from America into China by the Portuguese in the sixteenth century. *National Geographic Magazine*, April, 1927, p. 488.

[22] As to Central America, see D. G. Brinton, *supra*.

Mexico; and manufactured goods, such as textiles and pottery, were carried to Colombia by the Mayas in great trading canoes manned by twenty-five or thirty paddlers, and exchanged for emeralds and pearls.[23]

Like the wampum of North America and the bead money currency of Asia and Africa [24] shell beads served as currency in the active trade carried on between Peru and Nicaragua and the Isthmus of Panama. The Chimus on the north coast of Peru obtained the shells from which they made this money from Central America, and shells of certain varieties from Lower California and Central America are found in large quantities in the graves of Trujillo and Ancón.[25]

[23] Gregory Mason, *World's Work*, August, 1926, p. 439.
[24] Leo Wiener, *Africa and the Discovery of America*, Vol. II, pp. 236 et seq., 249 et seq.
[25] Wiener, *supra*, pp. 261, 264, citing Max Uhle, "La Esfera de Influencias del Pais de los Incas," from the *Revista Historica, Organo del Instituto Historico del Perú*, IV (1909), 22.

XIX

MAYA-CARIB CULTURE IN PERU

KIMMICH mentions many common customs and physical resemblances showing the relationship of the cultures of the Indians of the Peruvian coast (*Moches* in the north, —*Yungas* as a general term) with those of Mexico and Central America.

Both the Eteños (north Peruvian coast) and the Salibas (Carib stock of Venezuela and Colombia) had dances named after animals,—as deer, tiger, and turtle. The Salibas and the Moches began the year on the appearance of the constellation of Capricorn. The complexion of them all (Mayas, Caribs, and Yungas) was about the same,—a light brown. The Salibas and the Moches dressed their hair in the same way. The Salibas and Yungas both had the custom of weeping and making a great noise during an eclipse of the moon.

The Indians of Tumbes (north Peruvian coast) came originally from the Andes of Venezuela and Colombia, the home of the Salibas, and dressed the same as the Mayas and Caribs,—the women wearing a short skirt improvised from a square piece of cloth. The Mayas, the Chan-Chanes, and the Caribs used disks of tin as money. Both the Chanes (Yucatan) and the Chan-Chanes of Peru used great black pottery vessels as funerary urns. The

Chanes [1] and Yungas worshipped the moon. The Haitians (Caribs) and the Eteños venerated three magic stones of special virtue, respectively, in planting seed, in childbirth, and as assuring water and sunshine for the crops. Both the Haitians and the Pacasmayos (Peru) killed or cruelly mutilated medicine men who allowed their patients to die.[2]

The great terraced huacas, or irregular temple pyramids, from Chan-Chan to Lima, Pachacamac, and further south on the Peruvian coast, were dedicated to the same purpose and were of the same general type of construction,—although the material used was adobe either in bricks or in mass,—as the pyramids of Mexico and Central America.

Contact and kinship between the Moches (north Peruvian coast) and the Carib-Guaranis was shown by the identity of many words in the speech of both, e.g.: [3]

MOCHE	CARIB-GUARANI
mang (maize)	meng (maize)
mecha (hand)	mech (hand)
vira vira (cat-tail)	vira vira (cat-tail)
onek (one; note the same root as the English)	onik (one)

[1] The accidental similarity of *Chanes* and *Chinese* suggests an interesting inquiry into the meaning and origin of the word China, which was unknown to the people of that country,—called *Chin* and *Chintan* by the missionaries. Note the Aryan termination (*-an*, country; *t* for euphony, or possibly as a contraction of *te*, the) and the possible connection of *Chin* with the dragon or serpent in the worship of the people. *Chan* in Yucatan (Palenque) and in Peru was the sacred serpent or dragon.

[2] "Origen de los Chimus," *Bol. Soc. Geog. de Lima*, XXXIV (1918), 1st quarter, 60-65. This also reminds one of China.

[3] Kimmich, "Origen de los Chimus," *Bol. Soc. Geog. de Lima*, XXXIII (1917), 3rd quarter, 351-352.

PREHISTORIC "HIGH-PLACE" OF THE GOD

Temple and altar of sacrifice of the Coast Indians at Paramonga, Peru. It is of the same general type as the early altars and sacred high-places of Asia, Polynesia, and Mexico. The remains of lesser altars can be seen on the opposite side of the ravine.

Photograph from the air by W. O. Runcie.

MOCHE	CARIB-GUARANI
miss (cat)	michi (cat; the same word is used by the *gente* for cat in Peru today)
mo (this)	moe (this)
man (to eat; French *manger*)	min (to eat)
poto (a wide vase; note the English *pot*)	poto (thick)
moko (hump)	moko (hillock)
filo (seat)	milo (seat)

Chibcha-Moche relationship also appears in many words common to both, such as: [4]

MOCHE	CHIBCHA (COLOMBIA)
moisca (man)	moisk (man)
chach (baron)	chah (baron)
shi (moon)	chi (moon)
tsacal (of the night)	tsaca (night)

The same racial or, at least, linguistic strain is shown in many words common to the Moche and the Carib-Saliba, of which the following are examples: [5]

MOCHE	CARIB-SALIBA
nam (to fall)	name (to fall)
aja (lord)	aja (father)
javan (pig)	java (pig)
ech (what)	et ech (what)
faerr (year)	farro (year)
tsaeich (yours; Spanish *suyo*)	tsahaichi (yours)
amoss (no)	amo (no)

[4] Kimmich, *id.*, p. 352.
[5] Kimmich, *supra*, XXXIV (1918), 1st quarter, 45-46.

In the Zotohil dialect of the Quiché there are many words also found in related forms in the Moche,—such as:[6]

MOCHE	QUICHÉ
beñ (good; Spanish *bueno*)	ban (good)
fok (black)	ak (black)
be (road)	bei (road)
kor (maize; note the Aryan *corn*)	kor (maize)
pek (frog)	jek (frog)
mellu (egg)	mollo (egg)
iñ (I)	in (I)
chuch (laddie; Spanish *chico*)	chute (laddie)

Dr. Tello of Lima found stone carvings at Chavin-Huanta in the central Peruvian cordilleras which bear a marked resemblance to Mayan sculpture. "This style is notable for its æsthetic value which probably surpasses anything known from Peru, including even the monuments at Tiahuanaco."[7] Pottery excavated in the Chicama valley north of Trujillo is richly decorated with the typical conventional serpentine forms of Mayan art.[8]

Kroeber is of the opinion that this "Chavin Style" coast pottery is very old and contemporary with the Proto-Chimu. "The Proto-Chimu and Chavin styles not only are apparently the earliest but rank æsthetically the highest and the antecedents of both are unknown. With the passage of time more and more influences from and to a distance become discernible."[9]

---

[6] Kimmich, *supra*, XXXIII (1917), 3rd quarter, 357.

[7] A. L. Kroeber, *Ancient Pottery from Trujillo* (Field Museum of Natural History, Chicago, 1926), p. 37.

[8] See cuts in Kroeber, *supra*, pp. 38-39.

[9] Kroeber, *id.*, p. 42.

It is interesting to note in this connection that much of the pottery recently excavated by A. H. Verrill at Coclé, Panama,—of very old date as shown by the depth of the accumulations of soil covering it,—was decorated with the same technical conventional serpentine forms pictured on the Chicama pottery.[10]

[10] Mr. Verrill gives a brief description of his excavation at Coclé in *World's Work* for January, 1927. The pottery pictured in this article does not include the pieces just referred to. I do not know that the excellent drawings made by Mr. Verrill, which he kindly showed me, have been published.

XX

CHAN AND CHAN-CHAN

Ari, the title of the legendary Carib divine leaders and founders,—corresponding to the Ayars of Peru,—is preserved in the name of the Yunga village, *Arica,* at the mouth of an Andean quebrada where it debouches on the coast in southern Peru. (The place has been mentioned in events, lately, as seized by Chile in the "War of the Pacific," and the subject of the recent abortive plebiscitary undertaking.) It is possible that the same root is the basis of *Cari,*—the name of the earliest legendary white leader of a white race on Lake Titicaca,—and also of the name of the Carib race itself. In New Zealand the chief priest was called *Ariki.*[1]

The name of Chan-Chan, the great city of the Moches near Trujillo (Peru), also appears as a place-name in Ecuador near Guayaquil; and the name Moche itself reappears as far south as Chile, near Valdivia,—clearly marking points in the migration of the race.[2] The Chan-Chanes are said to have been a colony of the Chanes of Nachan on the river Chiapas, in southeastern Mexico, of Carib-Nahua stock. The words Chan-Chan and Nachan

[1] M. L.-D. De Rienzi, *Historia de la Oceania* (Barcelona, 1845, translated into Spanish from the French), p. 334. *Ante,* p. 131, n. 14.
[2] José Kimmich, *Bol. Soc. Geog. de Lima,* XXXIV (1918), 3rd quarter, 63.

AERIAL VIEW OF A PORTION OF THE RUINS OF CHAN-CHAN

The line through the right foreground is a track made by vehicles passing through the ruins.

Photograph by W. O. Runcie.

FRAGMENT OF A WALL OF THE SO-CALLED "CHIMU PALACE," IN
CHAN-CHAN, THE CHIMU CAPITAL

*From "Etnologia Peruana, Origen de los Chimus," by José
Kimmich. Boletín de la Sociedad Geográfica de Lima, 1918,
Tom. XXXIV, Trim. Prim., p. 57.*

Showing (often repeated) conventional figures of the sacred serpent and the
sacred falcon.

each signified "City of the Serpent," [3]—that is, of the serpent god of both peoples.[4]

A strong corroboration of the kinship of the two peoples is the constant recurrence, in the elaborate carvings on the adobe walls on the palace of the Grand Chimu at Chan-Chan, of the so-called "horizontal S" ($\backsim$),—conventional figure of the serpent,—the symbol of *Votan*.[5]

The worship of the serpent is pictured on the pottery of Chan-Chan. Many figures on the *huacos* have coiffures of coiled serpents adorned with feathers, typical of the cult of Quetzalcoatl.[6] Alternating with the serpent in the rich ornamentation of the Chimu's palace is line after line of conventional figures of the sacred bird of the race,

---

[3] Kimmich, *supra*, p. 64; *Popol Vuh*, p. cix, n. 2.

The same word,—spelled, by the archæologists exploring in Palestine, *Shan*, in *Beth-Shan*, recently excavated in northeast Palestine (formerly Canaan),—also meant serpent. *Beth-Shan* was the "house of the serpent," —in "the fortress home of the serpent god." As to the meaning of *Shan* and the excavation of *Beth-Shan*, see interview published in the press under date of February 10, 1929, with Dr. Alan Rowe, Director University of Pennsylvania Field Expedition. There is a school of archæologists and ethnologists who, if true to form, will claim that the identity in sound and meaning of the name of this ancient temple in Palestine with that of the Chimus on the north coast of Peru is merely accidental; but that theory is too great a tax on credulity. It cannot be repeated too often that the true explanation of such relationships is not that the one culture-word is derived from the other; but, rather, that both are derived from an older common Asiatic source.

Cf. Na-Chan (*na*, place; *Chan*, serpent), with China (*Chin*, or Shin; *na*).

The Central Asiatic origin of the culture of *Chan-Chan* appears in the same name of a ruined city (spelled *Shan-Shan*) discovered by Dr. Sven Hedin in Chinese Turkestan.

Mention of *Shanshan*, John Thomas Bealby, and Prince Peter A. Kropotkin, "Turkestan," *Encyc. Brit.*, 11th ed., XXVII, 425.

[4] The Chanes of Nachan claimed that their mythical chief, Votan, was the son of the serpent and their line of kings descended from him. Kimmich, *supra*, sec. e.

[5] Kimmich, *supra*, p. 64.

[6] Kimmich, *id.*

the divine falcon of both Manco Ccapac, founder of
Cuzco, and Vukub Cakix,—the priest or divine *Ara de
Feu* of the Quichés of Guatemala,—who caused the fire
"to descend from heaven upon the altar of sacrifices." [7]
The votive figure of the same sacred bird is also repeated
often on the temple gate of Tiahuanaco. The Colhuas,
farmers in the basin of Lake Titicaca, seem to have the
name as well as the serpent cult of the Colhuas who
taught agriculture to the primitive races of Mexico.[8]

The repetition on the walls of the palace of the Grand
Chimu of the sacred figures of the serpent and the falcon
was evidently intended to insure the blessing and protection of these gods. There is a primitive eloquence in this
pictured appeal. The sculpture becomes an act of devotion,—a cry for mercy which we can almost hear across
the desolation of the centuries.

These votive carvings seem to take a voice,—like the
endlessly repeated prayers in the prayer-wheels of the
Tibetans,—to the "jewel in the heart of the lotus." We
can feel with the Moches of Chan-Chan, as they crowded
to worship and the priests poured out the blood of the
sacrificial victim in the temple of the sun, the inherited
fear of disaster and destruction which hung over their
race.

No doubt the totems of the snake and the falcon in
their religious appeal, repeated so many times on the walls
of the palace, gave the people of Chan-Chan a sense of
security. It is true that for some centuries the Moches
enjoyed safety and freedom in this new land of Tlapallan.

[7] *Popol Vuh*, p. lxxx, n. 1.　Cf. Elijah.
[8] *Popol Vuh*, p. xxix, n. 3.

Their colony acquired riches and power. But the time came when the sacred symbols of the gods of their fathers did not stay the hand of the "giant" invaders from the sea, the conquest of the Inca, nor the fanatical destruction of the Spaniard.

The serpent and the eagle, so potent once in the rule of the Grand Chimu, seem all helpless now in the sand-blown heaps of tawdry ruins in the desert.

The ever-present hereditary fear of disaster, bred by racial experiences of flood, famine, pestilence, volcanic eruption, earthquake and war,—from which in generation after generation their race had fled in migrations into new lands (so vividly shown by the almost superhuman efforts put into the defensive works of Sacsahuaman, the location of Machu Picchu on its granite peak, the pitiful appeal to the serpent and the falcon, the constant pouring out of the blood of the victims as offerings to the gods),— was expressed in Chan-Chan by these sculptured prayers. Nevertheless the hand of tragedy fell upon the Moches.

XXI

THE PAINTED LAND

TLAPALLAN, the mythical cradle-land of the Nahua race, was spoken of by the Mexicans and Central Americans before the time of the Spanish conquest as the country bordering on the Caribbean in what is now northern Honduras.[1] This ancestral home was often identified in the local traditions with the sacred cradle-land, *Xibalba*, marked on the map published by Brasseur de Bourbourg as extending northwestward from Honduras, by the head of the Gulf of Honduras across the base of the peninsula of Yucatan, in what is now Guatemala, to the Chiapas River in southeastern Mexico.[2] The Toltec legend told of the origin of that people in the land of Huehue-Tlapallan and of their god Quetzalcoatl, a bearded white man, who taught them their arts, who at last "departed, some say, towards the unknown land of Tlapallan."[3]

Bourbourg makes some interesting suggestions, based on the study of the traditions as preserved in the several codices, as to the time of the colonization of the Nahua tribes (Chichimecs or Quinamés) in Tlapallan. "One finds marked by the sign Ce-Tecpatl (one flint) the re-

---

[1] Map, *Popol Vuh*, p. cxxxi.

[2] *Popol Vuh*, p. cxxxi.

[3] E. B. Tylor and Walter Lehmann, "Mexico: Ancient Civilization," *Encyc. Brit.*, 11th ed., *Popol Vuh*, p. lxiii, n. 3.

"*Tlapallan* is one of the most common synonyms of *Aztlan*. It must have been a city of importance since the Toltec astronomers met there and revised the calendar." T. S. Denison, *Mex. Ling.*, p. 139.

cital, although obscure, of the voyage of the Chichimeques (Colhuas)[4] to the country of Tlapallan,—the Colored or Painted Land, Huehue-Tlapallan of the Ancient Peoples. . . . The sign, One Flint, corresponds to a date more than three thousand years B.C."[5]

Tlapallan is said to be derived from *tlapalli*,—color for painting or something tinted.[6] *An* is the Aryan ending meaning place or land. Bourbourg, as just quoted, interprets Huehue-Tlapallan as the "colored (or tinted) land of the Ancient Peoples." This, no doubt, is in the sense of the land of origin, i.e., where the forefathers of the race lived. *Hue* in the Maya tongue meant egg.[7]

Huehue is probably merely the repetitive plural familiar in the American tongues,—sometimes used in the sense of emphasis. With the startling vividness of expression so often met in the American Indian speech, —the revelation of a profound insight into the philosophical essence of things, coupled with a rich imagination and an eloquent use of metaphor characteristic of the ancient Americans and the Asiatics,—the Nahua priests probably spoke of the land from which their race sprang as the racial egg-land,—the very birthplace and beginning from which they had been brooded.[8]

[4] *Int. Popol Vuh.*, lxviii.

[5] *Popol Vuh*, pp. lxiii-lxv. Bourbourg emphasizes his reasons for this conclusion in Note 1, page lxv, and says: "I suggest this idea as a simple hypothesis and with every reservation."

[6] *Id.*, p. lxiii, n. 3.

[7] *Dictionnaire Maya.* Note the same root in the Spanish *huevo*.

[8] This was somewhat the same conception as that of the modern scientists, —"everything begins in an egg"; but science today is by no means satisfied to stop at the egg, although it has not been able to go much further.

Bourbourg (*Popol Vuh*, p. lxiii, n. 3) recalls the various racial myths of man's creation from *red* clay, etc., and the sacred quality attached to *red*

The Mexican-Nahua myth and country of Tlapallan, the Painted Land, is perpetuated in the name of the present Peruvian department of Lambayeque,—formerly Llampallec.[9] Driven from Llapallan of Guatemala, preserving the memory of Huehue-Tlapallan, the ancient ancestral Painted Land,—in many stages by land and sea the emigrants sought a new land "where they could be free and worship their own gods." [10] How similar to the motives of our own ancestors in *their* emigration to America! "Sadly recalling in their songs" their ancient home [11] their leaders encouraged them with the promise of a new and rich land where they would make their home. The Peruvian tradition tells of their arrival in Lambayeque.

"In many balsas numerous foreigners, come from far countries across a wide expanse of sea, approached the shore and drew up their craft on the sandy beaches of

by both savage and civilized peoples. He mentions scarlet as "the sacred color of pontiffs and princes." He refers to figures painted in red on the royal tombs of Egypt and also in the grottoes and tombs of the Hindus and Etruscans; and recalls that Ezekiel speaks of "the images of the Chaldeans pourtrayed with vermilion" upon the wall of Babylon. The figure of the Inca painted on the apparently inaccessible face of the cliff overhanging Ollantaytambo is also red.

Huehue, the name of the "egg" land or ancient place of origin of the Nahua tribes (Chichimecs, Quinames, Colhuas), appears in Chinese Turkestan, ancient seat of the Aryan races and scene of successive wars between the whites and blacks. *Hui-Hui,* by Wilhelm Filchner (Berlin), 1928.

The original divine ancestor and leader of the first migrations told of in the traditions of the Polynesians, bore the same name, *Hui; Hui-te-rangiori.* Elsdon Best, *Polyn. Soc. Jour.* (1927), p. 347.

"It seems according to the very ancient [Chinese] writings that out of the original chaos there emerged an atom, an egg." Keith Henderson, *Prehistoric Man,* p. 219.

[9] M. C. Bonilla, "Llampallec," *Bol. Soc. Geog. de Lima,* XXXVI (1920), 4th quarter, 245.

[10] *Popol Vuh,* p. liii.

[11] *Popol Vuh, ibid.*

Aetin (Eten). Naimlap was their leader. He was accompanied by his wife, Ceterni, and many concubines. Among his servants were Pitazofi, his trumpeter who blew upon a seashell; Ninacolla, in charge of his throne and litter; Ninagentue, his cupbearer; Fongasigde, who was in charge of making roads of pounded shells; Ochocalo, the cook; Xam, the royal barber; and Llapchilutti, the chief tailor, skilled in feather work." [12]

The essentially Asiatic tone of Central American, Mexican, and Peruvian culture,—its gods, calendars and games; its strange compound of autocratic and popular government, the simple although effective organization based upon an absolute concentration of divine and temporal power in the "church" and the person of the chief; its delegation in equally concentrated form to the heads of subdivisions down to the point where the smallest village became a complete autonomy in its own orbit, balanced and held in its place in the social system by the "son of the sun" upon his throne,—was reflected in the elaborate organization of the retinue of Naimlap; like that (suggests Kimmich) of "an Asiatic Regulus,—a Hindu or Siamese-Burmese Raja, a Mongol or Mongoloid Khan." [13]

The style of the ancient art of the Nahua races, with its oriental richness of design and elaborate ornament, its elephants and mahouts, gods issuing from the mouths of wonder-beasts, its beast-masks, cobras de capello, dragons and sacred falcons of Asia,—fantastic monsters, grotesque figures produced in the teeming imagination of the East,

[12] M. C. Bonilla, *supra*, p. 247, citing Balboa, Cieza de Leon, Montesinos, Calancha, and many other chroniclers of the legend.
[13] "Origen de los Chimus," *Bol. Soc. Geog. de Lima*, XXXIV (1918), 1st quarter, 57.

—was carried to Peru in the durbar of the legendary potentate from Tlapallan, the "Painted Land." No doubt the voyage of Naimlap represents an actual occurrence of the early time,—but in the main it is but a type of a series of migrations of the varied branches of the ancient stock to new domains in the marvelous continent.

In the riches and freedom of the new land the old culture evolved distinctive forms. But, though modified by contact with other races,—and by the experiences of a new and exuberant life in the remarkable environment of the Andes and the Peruvian coast,—the decorated walls of Chan-Chan, the stone carvings of Chavin, the ornate pottery of Chimu and Nasca were characterized by the same religious talismans, the grotesque conceptions and even the conventional forms in technique of Toltec-Maya and Quiché art.

Religion, habits, customs, speech, ethnic and anthropological characteristics appear to indicate that among the various migrations which reached the beaches of Lambayeque were some of Maya culture. "The sea was their highway; knowledge of many things their equipment; feeble craft their vehicle; and the tradition of their long voyage passed on to posterity their history." [14]

The tradition speaks of balsas as the craft of this expedition by sea from the north,—such as are still in use by the Indians on this same coast, and such as Pizarro encountered coming up the coast under sail on his daring voyage to Peru. Similar rafts of balsa wood are familiar native means of down-river transportation in the interior on the Amazon River system. No doubt the great canoes

[14] Bonilla, *supra*, p. 246.

BALSA ON THE BEACH AT TALARA

Prehistoric type still in use. Note the section of a swordfish caught some miles off shore.

of the Nahuas, with their powerful crews of paddlers, accompanied the sailing rafts.

From Panama to the westernmost promontory of the southern continent, at Cape Blanco, the winds and currents aided them. *El Niño,* the Mexican current, rolled its vast volume towards the equator and aided the legendary adventurers from the north. Perhaps the voyagers kept in sight of the coast with its matted jungles crowding into the sea, its green forested mountains climbing steadily into the haze. Perhaps on some early dawn before the mists had formed they saw the glitter of the white crest of Chimborazo and the array of distant snow peaks in the Ecuadorean cordillera, glowing pink as they reflected the rays of the rising sun. Possibly these adventurers by sea had heard of the strange and different land beyond, the new Tula or Tlapallan, the earthly paradise their leaders had told them of, where it was neither cold nor hot,—a new Avalon "where falls not hail, or rain, or any snow, nor ever wind blows loudly."

No doubt they advanced by stages and camped at times in various places. As they reached the low black reefs of Parina Point a new scene arose. The dense forest and jungles had disappeared. The land was clear and open. The air was crowded with new species of sea birds. Great seals and sea-lions crowded in dense colonies on the rocky islets. Vast schools of strange fish swarmed upon the surface of the sea for miles. Now they were no longer aided by the winds and currents. A cold and steady drift from the south retarded them. The prevailing wind was against them. It seemed to be a completely new and pleasing world abounding in plenty.

Pressing on but a little way, the travelers saw the serried ranks of the Peruvian Andes crowding to the beach, flinging out bold headlands towards the beating surf,—bare ridges crossed and marked by the wind in myriad delicate patterns of form and color, running down to the sea like huge flying buttresses bracing at right angles the main sierras which loomed beyond at immense and indefinite heights in a lucent amethyst veil. Perhaps it was in the "winter" season of *garúas* and the middle slopes had taken on the marvelous rich green of the small seasonal herbage of amancaes and transient grasses. The nearer hills were clothed in exquisite tints,—deep red, soft browns, ochre, and the delicate shades of mauve, like finely tanned leather,—of that inexpressible smoothness of surface texture which only exists where the soft disintegration of the soil by the air is seldom disturbed by washing rains.

In the distance illuminated sierras rose range on range, violet mists filled the quebradas in a far perspective of lights and shadows. It was Tlapallan,[15] the *Painted Land*. One can imagine the joy with which Naimlap and his people drew up their boats upon the gravelly beach and gazed in wonder on the panorama of the Purple Mountains.

[15] Now Lambayeque,—the Aryan substantive terminal *an* changed to the adjectival *eq*.

XXII

A GUATEMALAN AYAR MANCO CCAPAC

In the Nahuatl myth, as in the Scandinavian, men were
created in three castes, the first containing the nobles,
priests, and soldiers, the second the free artisans, and the
third the slave laborers.[1] Both legends are obviously of
Asiatic origin.

According to the Nahuatl legend, their tribe was almost
entirely destroyed by a hurricane and by a deluge. After
this, when their race had recuperated its strength, they
schemed to throw off the yoke of the neighboring Colhuas
to whom they had been subject. The *Ara* (Ayar?) *Vukub-
Cakix*, a giant and demigod, appears as the powerful
chief of the Colhuas in the country of Tlapallan adjoining that of the Nahuas.[2] *Vukub-Cakix* boasted that he
was "the equal of the sun and the moon,"—which indicates that the Colhuas in Guatemala, as their descendants
on Lake Titicaca, worshipped these luminaries. *Vukub-
Cakix* had two sons: *Zipacna*, who formed the mountains
and "raised the volcanoes of Guatemala in one night";
and *Cabrakan*, who caused the earth to tremble and "by
his mere will could overthrow the heaven and the earth."

The Hurricane raises up two brothers to aid the Nahuas
against *Vukub-Cakix* and his sons. The champions of
the Nahuas were "the two *Hun-Ahpu*." They are rep-

[1] *Popol Vuh*, p. cxxiv, n. 1; p. 199 *et seq.*
[2] *Popol Vuh*, pp. cxxiii, cxxvii.

resented as "serpents," evidently in reference to their magical powers. They could only hope to overcome *Vukub-Cakix* by "ruse and perfidy." This they did and put out his eyes and despoiled him of his great riches. The *Hun-Ahpu* were aided by "four hundred young men," and they enticed the sons of *Vukub-Cakix* into their power by appealing to their ravenous appetites.

Zipacna was induced to enter a cave in search of a "monstrous crawfish made by their enchantments." While he was in the cave the *Hun-Ahpu* closed it up by causing the rocks of the mountain to fall, and converted *Zipacna* into stone. *Cakabran* was overcome while "gorged with food and drink." [3]

This fable evidently refers to a long struggle between the Nahuas and their kinsmen the Colhuas. It has many of the features of the Peruvian Paccari-Tampu myth, e.g., the brother who was induced to enter the cave and was there imprisoned; the brother who was turned into stone; and the brother who had the power, by his mere will, to overthrow and cast up mountains.

There is a more rational tradition preserved by *Ixtlil-txochitl* [4] which may have been the basis of the fable. The *Nahuas*, in order to put an end to the oppression and tyranny which they had suffered from the *Colhuas*, evidently disguising their resentment, had invited the most famous of the *Quinamés* (*Colhuas*) to a feast and overcame their oppressors after the latter had become drunk and gorged with food. [5]

[3] *Popol Vuh*, pp. cxxvi, cxxvii.
[4] *Histoire des Chichimèques*, I, chap. 1.
[5] *Popol Vuh*, p. cxxvii.

"It was perhaps tribes of that race [*Colhuas*], overcome by the stratagem of the Nahuas, who emigrated some centuries before our era to South America, whither they carried the cult of the sun, represented by the *Ara*, son of Heaven [*Vukub-Cakix, Ara*, seven times the color of fire], which some travelers think they have recognized in the head of the parrot or the condor sculptured on the monolithic gate of Tiahuanaco in Peru." [6] *Vukub-Cakix's* title,—*Ara*,—appears to be the same as that of Manco Ccapac, the Ayar who came from Paccari-Tampu to establish the rule of the Ayar race at Cuzco. Like the Ayars of Cuzco, the *Ara, Vukub-Cakix*, was a worshipper, priest, and descendant of the sun.[7]

The symbols and totems of *Vukub-Cakix* were the same as those of the kings of Cuzco,—the sun itself and the falcon or eagle, the divine bird whose *Huaco* Manco Ccapac carried in the sacred hamper. In most of the Veraguan graves,—attributed by Bourbourg to the *Vitznahuas*, "worshippers of the *Ara, Vukub-Cakix*,"—the sacred idols of the eagle, small images of the divine bird, "about four inches from wing to wing," were found around the necks of the dead.[8]

The corresponding symbol of the Peruvian falcon appears many times on the monolithic gate of Tiahuanaco in the form of a man with a falcon's head, like the Egyptian *Ré* and *Vishnu* of the Indo-Aryans.

[6] *Popol Vuh*, p. cxxviii.
[7] *Popol Vuh*, p. lxxx, n. 1; pp. cxxvi, 31-33.
[8] W. Bollaert, *Antiquities, etc.*, of South America, pp. 30-31.

XXIII

THE PACCARI-TAMPU MYTH IN MEXICO

The Paccari-Tampu myth of Peru, in which four Ayar leaders and their sister-wives came out of caves, or "windows," to found a dynasty at Cuzco, has its counterpart in Mexico and Central America.

In Peru, some writers have claimed, it was after the destruction of the ancient kingdom of the megalithic builders,—when the nucleus of the Ayar race which survived had recuperated its strength and numbers in what is supposed to have been the fastnesses of the Vilcapampa, —that these new founders appeared.[1] Professor Bingham sought for Paccari-Tampu in the Vilcapampa.[2]

However, the Paccari-Tampu myth was a myth of the origin of the Ayar race and told of the first appearance of the ancestors of the Incas. They came from caves or "windows" and settled at Cuzco. They were the first "Civilizers," taught agriculture and a settled mode of life, and selected the site of Cuzco on account of the richness of the soil.

The first king mentioned in the Ayar traditions,—Pirua Paccari Manco,—gave his name, *Paccari*, to the mythical locality from which he came. The second was Manco Ccapac. It is evidently to *Paccari* Manco and to his son Manco Ccapac and the establishment of the latter at Cuzco

[1] Markham, *Incas of Peru*, pp. 48-57.
[2] *Inca Land*, p. 312 *et seq.*

that the myth relates. These founders of the Ayar line in Cuzco had probably themselves inherited the myth from a far earlier time.

According to the authentic traditions carefully preserved by the professional historians of the race, eighty-five Ayar kings (twenty-one of them ruling in Tampu-Tocco during the exile from Cuzco) succeeded Pirua Paccari Manco before the Ayar Manco extended his rule from Tampu-Tocco and gradually reestablished the Ayar authority at Cuzco.

Paccari-Tampu (the Tavern of the Dawn) was an ancestral myth of the primitive Ayar people. It referred to a distant time when under certain leaders they had given up cave life, taken to agriculture, developed the arts, become civilized, and carried their civilization to other peoples.

The residence of early man in caves is one of the most familiar features of his rise. The origin of certain tribes in caves is a widely distributed tradition in Asia. "The Neolithic caves are widely spread throughout Europe, and have been used as the habitations and tombs of the early races who invaded Europe from the East with their flocks and herds."[3] Undoubtedly before reaching Europe the ancestors of these peoples had lived in caves in Asia.

If the site of this cave life of the remote ancestors of the Ayar race and the location of the mythical Paccari-Tampu is to be sought, it is more likely to be found in the mountains of Turkestan than in the hills about Cuzco. The "Tavern of the Dawn" is the typical poetic speech of

[3] W. B. Dawkins, "Cave," *Encyc. Brit.*, 11th ed., V, 577.

the imaginative Proto-Aryan people and suggests the Aryan god of the sky, of the light, and of the sun.

The title or descriptive name Paccari, as applied to the early chief, means the "first or original ancestor." Paccari-Tampu, the ancestral tavern or *tambo*, would indicate the cradle-land of the race.

However, as in all such myths among all races, the Paccari-Tampu myth of migration and early chieftainship constantly tends to become a myth of creation. Pirua Paccari Manco becomes the Son of the Sun, and *Paccari-Tampu*, in the flowery language of the ancient Ayars, is the "Tavern of the Dawn,"—the place from which the sun first rose.

"The Achachilas are also the *Paccarinas* or ancestors of the Ayllu or the tribe." [4]

With all the veneer of Christian Catholicism the worship of these family ancestors is today, as it was in pre-Spanish times, the most intimate religion of the Peruvian Indians. They still see the *Achachilas* or *Paccarinas* (spirits of their dead ancestors or "Grandfathers") in every prominent mountain height. As Jew or Christian makes his homage to *Father Abraham*, the Quichua traveler embodies his prayer to Pirua Paccari Manco in the stone which he places upon the sacrificial pile where the trail crosses the summit of the mountain.

In the Quiché myth of Guatemala, after the destruction of the race by a deluge, "comes the creation of the four men and their wives who are the ancestors of the Quichés, and the tradition records the migrations of the

---

[4] Adolph F. Bandelier, *The Islands of Titicaca and Koati*, p. 154, n. 112. Italics mine. M. P.

nation to Tulan, otherwise called the Seven Caves, and thence across the sea, whose waters were divided for their passage." [5]   The Maya traditions also, like the Peruvian and the Quiché, tell of "four famous chiefs or ancestors." [6]

As the Peruvian Ayar Manco Ccapac unwinds his sling from his head and casts a stone to each of the cardinal points,—announcing that in this manner he takes possession of the four quarters of the earth,—likewise in Mexico the legendary Chichimec prince took possession of the valley of Anahuac. [7]

The Peruvian Paccari-Tampu myth, the caves or windows or doors of the "Tavern of the Dawn" from which came the four Ayar brothers, ancestors of the Inca race, is evidently a version of the same archaic tradition from which the Polynesians derived the myth of *Hawaiki-rangi,*—the sacred building which stood on the summit of the "Mountain of Rites" in *Irihia,* the traditional ancestral home of the Polynesians.   From its four doors which opened to the four cardinal points of the compass the original ancestors passed in their migrations to the four quarters of the earth.   "These are the ways by which separated the offspring of Tane-nui-a-Rangi." [8]

[5] E. B. Tylor, "Mexico, Ancient History," *Encyc. Brit.,* 11th ed.; Brasseur de Bourbourg, ed., *Popol Vuh,* p. xci. This reference to Tulan, "the Land of Reeds," seems to be of Asiatic origin. It is evidently of extreme antiquity, and refers to the very earliest migrations beyond the seas, and thence across the seas to America. The event was so ancient that the means of passage seem to have been forgotten, and is explained by the magic of the "division of the waters for their passage."

[6] Tylor, *supra.*

[7] Brasseur de Bourbourg, *Popol Vuh,* p. ccxlii, n. 2. "Chicomoztoc, 'the seven caves.' This is one of the most important of the Aztlan names." T. S. Denison, *Mexican Linguistics,* p. 136.

[8] Elsdon Best, "Irihia," *Polyn. Soc. Jour.,* 1927, pp. 338-340. The "Tavern of the Dawn" reminds one of the "Dawn Man" (*Eoanthropus*) of Smith Woodward and Henry Fairfield Osborn.

XXIV

CHRONOLOGY

BESIDES the archaic migrations which brought corn, place-names, racial names and descriptive words, and structure of common speech from Mexico to Peru,—and perhaps a movement of primitive man along the same lines from north to south even earlier than this,—there appears to have been an archaic movement of the megalithic race from Asia to the Pacific islands and thence to the American continent. This migration, which no doubt consumed many centuries, has left its most striking monuments in the Carolines, in Easter Island, and in the Peruvian Andes. This culture was so old that neither the Polynesians nor the Peruvians at the time of their discovery by the Europeans had any knowledge of the builders of the megalithic structures.

In both Peru and Polynesia the trained minstrels and historians had preserved the chronicles of the people from very remote times. But neither on the islands nor on the continent did the memory of man, as preserved and perpetuated in these traditions, run far enough back to account for the quarrying and transportation of the immense stones over long distances, the Cyclopean masonry, or the art by which they had been carved and fitted with so much nicety, for the immense walls, harbors, palaces, temples and fortresses; nor for the origin or description of the race which had left these imperishable monuments of its power. Even today these stupendous structures seem rather the work of supermen, or demigods, than of men.

The carefully preserved traditions of Peru, as given to the earliest Spanish chroniclers by the *Quipucamayocs* and *Amautas*,—the trained recorders with quipus, or knotted cords, and the professional legend-bearers who preserved and passed on by word of mouth the story of the race from one generation to another,—covered a period variously estimated by the chroniclers and later historians as from 2,000 to 3,000 years before the arrival of Pizarro in Peru; and yet none of these traditions undertook to account for the building of Sacsahuaman, Tiahuanaco, or Ollantaytambo.

These megalithic works were older than tradition. They, in the opinion of the author, were the work of a white Paleo-Aryan stock[1] which has left traces of its physical type and of its language in Polynesia and Peru even to this day. No other race than the white race has ever attained the capacity required for such stupendous accomplishments. These Cyclopean builders were probably among the ancestors of the Caucasian types found by the first European explorers in more or less purity in Polynesia and Peru. But this Paleo-Aryan megalithic race belongs to so remote an epoch that its own descendants in Polynesia and Peru in the sixteenth century knew nothing of it. It was not only prehistoric but pre-traditional. The erection of the great megalithic struc-

[1] Controlling and directing the labor of the indigenous people. See authorities, *infra*.

XXXIII

POTTERY

IN ceramics, the Quichuas and Aymarás of the mountains, the Mochics and Nascas on the coast, attained a high degree of excellence, but not to the same superlative degree as in other arts. The enameled porcelain of China, the glazed pottery of Persia and Egypt, the glass of Venice displayed a higher art in the finish and texture of the vessels and the refinement of their ornamentation and design than the pottery of Peru. Nevertheless much of the burned ware of Chan-Chan, Nasca, and Cuzco is not far inferior to that of Asia and Europe.

Much of the Peruvian pottery is of fine texture, smoothly finished and burned in what is almost equal to a glaze, in many shapes of graphic and artistic design. The pottery differs between different epochs and localities. That of Cuzco and Machu Picchu, in its grace and simplicity of line, strongly resembles the pottery of the Greeks. Much of this,—lamps, mugs, pitchers,—without ornamentation, of a brown smooth finish, is extremely attractive. Beautiful vases, dishes, and cups of wood were carved at Cuzco and painted in excellent colors, with graphic representations of battle and adventure.

As writing was early suppressed, the records of pottery and other utensils are extremely valuable for the light they throw on the manners and customs, clothing, arms, and religious practices of the people. Most of the pottery of the coast, or Yungas, is elaborately ornamented with a high technical and artistic skill, both in the forms in which it is molded, and in the painting burned into the vessel in red, black, white, or blue. The jugs are of an infinite variety of forms,—some "portrait" figures, most lifelike and expressive representations of individuals,—some representing comic scenes in family or neighborhood life, striking figures of gods, birds, fishes, or animals, many lifelike in the extreme, others exaggerated to absurd caricatures, or fantastic conceptions of "futurist" art.

Much of the pottery, either in its shape or molding or in its painted decoration, is of a symbolic religious character. Some is decorated in conventional forms of art whose original signification is scarcely recognizable; other examples,—especially the painted decorations of geometric patterns emblematic of ancient esoteric and totemic rituals, —are of religious significance. "Perhaps one of the most interesting coincidences is the occurrence of another form of cross, the Swastika. While this type is not seen often in the architecture, it occurs in almost every form of the potter's art which has been excavated from the first epoch of Tiahuanacu's ruins. If the capital has the age some students claim for it, here are some of the first examples obtainable of the use of this well-known good-luck or religious symbol. It is worthy of serious study and occurs so often in Tiahuanacu ceramics that ample examples are available."[1] The swastika cross "was used as a religious emblem in India and China at least ten centuries before

[1] Stewart E. McMillin, "Swastika Cross at Tiahuanaco," *West Coast Leader*, March 29, 1927.

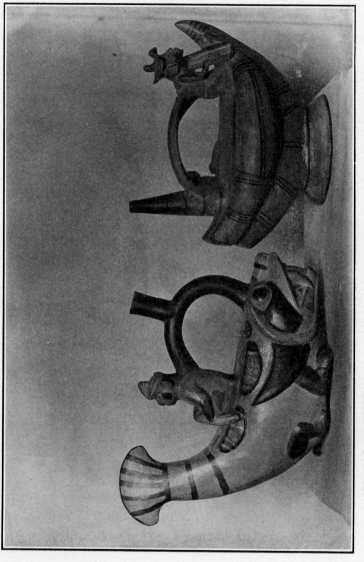

HUACOS, PREHISTORIC POTTERY FROM A GRAVE, NORTH COAST OF PERU

HUACO. PREHISTORIC POTTERY FROM A GRAVE, NORTH COAST OF PERU

Fanciful representation of a llama.

the Christian era and is met with on Buddhist coins and inscriptions from various parts of India." [2]

A large section of Peruvian pottery is devoted to pornographic art whose vivid representations indicate that the forms of vice practiced in decadent Rome were not unknown to the Incas. In this is clearly written one of the causes of the decline of the old megalithic race. [3]

[2] Thomas M. Fallow, "Cross," *Encyc. Brit.*, 11th ed. The swastika cross appears frequently in the figured ornamentation of rugs bought by the author in the Andes. This archaic talisman is probably a conventional representation of the human figure, on one knee, with arm uplifted in suppliance to God. In itself it is a constant prayer.

[3] It was but a type of an early Asiatic degeneracy (Genesis 19, 4-8). The reproaches of the Inca reformers recall the condemnations of Moses (Leviticus 18:22, 23, 27) and the anathemas of St. Paul (Romans 1:26, 27). Though it left no such record, a similar cause may have contributed to the decline of the archaic civilization of England, also of oriental origin, so graphically pictured by Massingham. As for the alleged effect of similar degeneracy in contemporary India, see *Mother India*, by Katherine Mayo.

XXXIV

LETTERS AND STEEL

ONE of the puzzling mysteries of Peru has always been connected with the *tools* with which the artisans of the megalithic age cut the stones which are fitted with such perfection into the incomparable masonry of the temples, forts, and palaces of the Andes.

The fortress of Sacsahuaman, the high altar of Ollan-taytambo, the ashlar temple of Pisac, the royal tomb and sacred wall of Machu Picchu, the convents and temple of the sun at Cuzco, though of a crude architectural plan, are constructed of masonry of such nicety and perfection as perhaps has never been excelled anywhere else in the world. The stones,—some of them of colossal size,—are cut and joined in a perfect and mortarless union as though they had been *molded* into the corresponding angles and curves. Some are of hard porphyry, others of softer limestone (Sacsahuaman); but they are all shaped to their place in the curving, sloping or rectilinear walls as though they had been fitted together in some *plastic* material by a master mason who combined the talents of a mathematician and an artist.

It is obviously impossible that this work of super-art, which is at least equal to the best examples of the masonry of the Orient, of Greece, or of modern times, could have been accomplished merely with *stone* cutting tools. These blocks were undoubtedly cut with metal bits, tempered to a hard edge.   Many bronze chisels have been found in the huacas but these are said to be easily dulled when tested in rock-cutting.[1] Some of these tools contained ninety-four parts of copper to six of tin.[2] Emerald, one of the hardest of stones,—obtained by the Peruvians in considerable quantities from the desert of Atacama in the south, as well as from Colombia,—was carved with ease and precision by the Peruvians.[3]

In the cataclysm of the conquest and subsequent exploitation of the Indians by the Spaniards, many native arts were undoubtedly lost; and processes of tempering bronze so as to produce a hard cutting edge, which may have been known to the Peruvians when their country was overrun by the Spanish adventurers, may have been concealed by them from their oppressors and subsequently lost.   They were acquainted with alloys and are said to have hardened their bronze by the mixture of a small part of gold with copper and tin,—producing an alloy called *chumpi*.   Seventy-five per cent of the world's supply of vanadium,—one of the most effective ingredients for hardening steel,—comes from Peru; but it is not known that the ancient Peruvians had any knowledge of its use.

However, the megalithic masonry of Peru was a lost art long before the arrival of the Spaniards.   The matchless walls of Cuzco, even those that did not belong to the

---

[1] *Peruvian Antiquities*, Rivero and Tschudi, translated by Francis L. Hawks, New York, 1853, p. 230.

[2] Alexander von Humboldt, *Vues des Cordillères* (Paris, 1816), Vol. I, p. 314.

[3] Prescott, *Conquest of Peru*, I, 125-26.

megalithic age, had been constructed in the flowering of
an art which had long since, like other arts of the Peruvians, fallen into decay, as had the American race itself,
not only in Peru but in many other parts of the hemisphere. In many places there were the remains of cultures in both North and South America of which the inhabitants of the country, at the time of the arrival of the
Europeans, had no knowledge and sometimes not even a
tradition.

Nearly everywhere, however, there existed the tradition of a superior *white* race who had brought an ancient
culture and erected the great monuments. The well-pre-
served Peruvian tradition was that the stone structures
at Quinoa and Huaytara had been built by "bearded white
men" with *iron tools*.[4] Like much of its culture, the white
race itself had disappeared,—lost in the flood of the
"darker peoples,"—just as it had in India, Polynesia, and
China in varying degrees, notwithstanding the restrictions
of caste established for its protection.

The purity of the ancient religion, its worship of an
omnipotent, invisible, and immortal God,—as among the
Jews, Hindus, and Egyptians,—was corrupted by the worship of idols and perverted by lust. Some trace of the
white Ayars still survived in the noble castes, and the mixture of their blood can be seen even today among the
Serranos.[5] The main features of the pre-Ayar social organization still preserved the marvelous industry of the
people at the time of the Spanish conquest; but the race
itself, its character, and its culture were in a state of decadence.

[4] Brasseur de Bourbourg, *Popol Vuh*, pp. ccxxiii-ccxxiv.
[5] As to the *white* natives of Chachapoyas, see Cieza de Leon, *La Crónica
del Perú* (Madrid, 1922), p. 259.

Letters had been lost. The art of writing by pictures and perhaps by conventional characters had once existed.[6] In the reign of Huanacauri Pirua [7] "The Amautas who know the events of those times by very ancient traditions, passed from hand to hand, say that when this prince was reigning there were letters, and also men very wise in them called *Amautas,* and that these men taught reading and writing. The principal science was astrology. As far as I am able to learn, they wrote on the leaves of the plantain tree which they dried and then wrote upon."

The Amauta king, Titu Yupanqui Pachacuti, was defeated and killed in the pass of Vilcanota (La Raya) by invaders from the south,—"ferocious men," who also "had some black men among them." [8] The Cuzco dynasty was overthrown, the kingdom of the Amautas overrun, much of the ancient culture lost, and the dark ages enveloped Peru for hundreds of years.[9]

[6] Montesinos, *Memorias Antiguas* (Hak. Soc., London, 1920), pp. 18, 62.

[7] The third of the "proto-historic" kings of Cuzco, listed by Montesinos. Means (Note to *Memorias Antiguas,* p. xlvi) places his date at about 200 A.D. However, the beginning of the white Pirua-Ayar culture of southern Peru, represented by this legendary chief, was no doubt much earlier than the date given by Means.

[8] The traditions state that the king, contrary to the advice of his officers, left his fortifications in the pass,—which, properly defended, should have been impregnable,—and went out to meet the invaders in the open. He sacrificed discretion and strategy to his personal bravery. (Montesinos, *supra,* p. 61.)

[9] A number of engraved wooden tablets discovered some years ago on Easter Island are described (figures in part reproduced) in the *Journal of the Polynesian Society.* Dr. A. Carroll of Sidney has published in the *Journal,* Vol. I (1892), pp. 102, 233, an account of the same in which he gives extensive translations therefrom. The authenticity and reliability of Dr. Carroll's translations have been questioned by William Churchill (*Easter Island*). Nevertheless Dr. Carroll's standing among Polynesian students and in the pages of the *Journal of the Polynesian Society* as a learned student of ethnology and particularly of Polynesian antiquities entitles his statements to the most careful consideration.

As to the question of communication between Polynesia and the western coast of South America it is most interesting to note that the translations

Centuries later, when the ancient religion, which had meanwhile been nurtured in the remote fastnesses of the Vilcapampa, was reestablished by the survivors of the Ayars, an effort was made to revive the art of writing; but a reactionary priest, true to certain types of the clerical party, persuaded the king to proscribe it, under penalty of death.

Tupac Cauri, Pachacuti VII,[10] "began to pull his forces together and to recover some cities and provinces, but, as

of the Easter Island hieroglyphics given by Dr. Carroll are accounts of Quichua and Aymará history and of religious observances in the Andes. Furthermore it should be noted that the religion and the mode of expression of the sun-worshippers and the history of the "sun-fires" of the Andean people, as given in Dr. Carroll's translations, correspond to a remarkable degree with what is known of the beliefs and mode of expression of the pre-Columbian Peruvians.

The Easter Island hieroglyphics are conventionalized figures of eagles, serpents, and men, and parts of same, in various positions and combinations, carved on wooden tablets. The figures are protected from erasure by friction by ridges or raised lines carved or left on the tablets.

The subject is discussed by J. Park Harrison, *Hieroglyphics of Easter Island* (London, 1874), and W. J. Thompson, U.S.N., *Te-Pito-te-henua* (Smithsonian Institution, 1891).

"In a house of the Sun called Poquen-Cancha, which is near Cuzco, they [the Incas] had the life of each of the Yncas with the land they conquered painted with figures on certain boards, and also their origin." Christóval de Molina, *Fables and Rites of the Incas*, Hak. Soc., 1873, p. 4, cited in *The Islands of Titicaca and Koati* by Adolph F. Bandelier, pp. 311-12.

"And after he [the great Pachacuti Inca Yupanqui] had ascertained the most notable of their ancient histories, he had it all painted after its order on large boards and he placed them in a big hall in the House of the Sun." Sarmiento, cited by Bandelier, *ibid.*, p. 313.

The Mongols also kept written records on small boards or tablets. Sir Henry Yule, *Book of Marco Polo*, p. 352. These were very similar to those kept by the Easter Islanders.

The tradition of Easter Island was that the "hymns, songs, genealogies and traditions,"—"like the seabirds and the nets,"—came from the East. J. Macmillan Brown, *The Riddle of the Pacific*, p. 79.

[10] Seventy-eighth king of Ayar blood in Montesinos' list. Means, on Montesinos' data, calculates 1300 A.D. as the beginning of his reign. This event was long before the rise of the Inca dynasty, and no doubt was much earlier than the date mentioned.

FRONT VIEW OF A DOUBLE-CHAMBERED WATER-JUG FROM
CHAN-CHAN (NORTH COAST OF PERU)

From a drawing by Joseph Anthony Atchison.

(See reverse side for description)

FRONT VIEW OF A DOUBLE-CHAMBERED WATER-JUG FROM CHAN-CHAN (NORTH COAST OF PERU)

It represents a Priest wearing a miter of Asiatic type. He is offering a written prayer to the Chi-mu gods,—the Falcon and the Serpent. The custom of presenting prayers in writing exists in Asia, e.g., the Tibetan prayer-wheels, where emphasis is given to the appeal to the Deity by many revolutions of a wheel containing the written prayer. This prehistoric jug shows writing in Peru in the process of evolution from hieroglyphic picture representations. The upright bars in pairs repeated four times are conventional representations of the scepter of power which always appears in both hands of the idols of the supreme Deities. The serpentine character is the Sacred Serpent. The figure resembling a reversed C repeated four times probably represents the Sacred Falcon. Of significance is the identity of this character with the Egyptian Demotic sign of the Sacred Falcon— (9 Encyc. Brit. 11th ed., p. 65.) Below is a tax-collector (probably temple official) with his money-sack and staff of office. The entire scene represents a dedication of the collection to the gods,—much as the preacher in our churches holds the collection plate aloft and offers it to God. The whole inscription is as though the ancient worshippers said over and over again: "Oh, Holy and Sacred Serpent and Falcon, save us and help us; for thine is the kingdom and the power and the glory (scepter) for ever and ever."

Huaco presented to the author by Mr. Floyd Sears, formerly United States Consular Agent at Salaverry, Peru.

the people obeyed him with so little certainty and as they were so greatly corrupted in the matter of religion and customs, he took steps to conquer them, because he said that if these people communicated with his own they would corrupt them with the great vices to which they had given themselves up like wild beasts. Therefore he tactfully sent messengers in all directions, asking the chiefs to put a stop to superstition and the adoration of the many gods and animals which they adored; and the outcome of this was but a slight mending of their ways and the slaying of the Ambassadors.[11]

"The King dissembled for the time being and made great sacrifices and appeals to Illatici Huira Cocha. One reply was that the cause of the pestilence had been the

---

[11] This struggle of the leaders to preserve the true religion is like a page from the Bible. The troubles of the Quichuas, as of the Israelites, were said to be due to the worship of false gods and idols. The constant appeal of the greatest of their kings and their influential women, like Mama Ciuaco, the mother of the great Rocca (Montesinos, *supra*, pp. 68-9) was that the people should leave their bestiality and return to the worship of the true Ayar god, Viracocha,—who, in all essentials, was the same omnipotent spirit as our own God. All through the chronicles appears the thought, like the imprecations of the Prophets of the Jews, that disaster and death were the penalty of apostasy, blessings and power the reward of fidelity to the true god.

With the same psychology as our own Puritans, *they burned witches*. (It is now said that our Puritans only *drowned* them.) "Sinchi Roca, the fifth Inga, was very sagacious and he always endeavored to enforce the laws of his ancestors. At this time, abominable wickedness was very general; the kings did little about it, not wishing to impart (knowledge of) it to their vassals. Those who most deeply regretted it were the women. Their anger arrived at such a level that they ordered many men to be killed by witchcraft, an evil of which they made use by means of seers and wizards, who also were very wicked men. This was carried so far that they killed many important persons. Inga Sinchi Roca ordered a meeting to be held, and the members of it determined that the ancient laws should be observed, and they commanded that death by burning with the instruments of their witchcraft should be meted out not only to the wizards but also to those who commanded them to kill others, and this penalty was promptly carried out upon the guilty, who were many."

letters, and that no one ought to use them nor resuscitate them, for, from their employment, great harm would come. Therefore Tupac Cauri commanded by law that, under the pain of death, no one should traffic in *quilcas*, which were the parchments and leaves of trees on which they used to write, nor should use any sort of letters. They observed this oracular command with so much care that after this loss the Peruvians never used letters. And, because in later times a learned amauta invented some characters, they burnt him alive, and so, from this time forth, they used threads and *quipos*." [12]

In the great convulsion and the degeneracy which followed the overthrow of Titu Upanqui, much of the ancient culture besides letters was no doubt lost,—possibly including the perfection of the art of the prehistoric masonry and the knowledge of the tools by which it was wrought. The unfinished condition of some of the greatest of the monuments, the scattered material along the Inclined Way at Ollantaytambo, the wild confusion and disorder of the high place itself, tell of the sudden disaster which fell upon the workmen, the precipitancy with which they dropped their tools and fled or were slaughtered where they stood. It is not impossible that the ancient builders,—whose works would never have been believed possible but that their imperishable solidity and excellence have preserved them as bodily evidence of an achievement which otherwise all the archæologists would have proved to be preposterous,—had steel tools.

Montesinos chronicles the tradition that in the reign

[12] Montesinos, *supra*, p. 64.

of the Ayar Tacco Capac [13] Peru was invaded by giants who came by the sea. Some of them settled at Huayatara and Quinoa in the highlands above Ica, and Montesinos repeats the tradition that they completed some buildings, which they found begun, with the *instruments of iron* which they had brought with them from their own land.[14]

The scouts of Ayar Tacco Capac also reported that "very large and tall men" had landed in the north about Santa Elena "and were ruling that land from Puerto Viejo [so called by the Spanish chronicler of the tradition] and that the natives of it were fleeing from them because they used their bodies so ill, and in my opinion it was not that they fled from the sin, for they themselves had it also, but that they fled from the *danger of the instrument with which the giants took their lives.*"[15] This reference is somewhat enigmatic but it would seem to refer to a weapon of metal, probably a sword or knife; and as bronze and copper had long been known to the Peruvians, it must have been some new and deadlier blade, possibly steel, with which the giant invaders terrified the Indians of the coast.

Prescott quotes Ondegardo and Herrera as saying that the Peruvians had no tools of iron or steel and reflects

[13] Given by Means (Int. to Montesinos, *supra*) as 275 A.D., but probably much earlier. Brasseur de Bourbourg (Int. to *Popol Vuh*, p. ccxxiv) estimates the date of this invasion as 1500 B.C.

[14] Montesinos, *supra*, p. 41.

[15] Montesinos, *supra*, p. 41. Italics mine. M. P.

Cieza de Leon, one of the best of the early observers, says that the Peruvians practiced sodomy publicly (*supra*, pp. 173, 182), and that even at the time of the Spanish conquest boys dressed as women were kept professionally in the temples for this purpose (*ibid.*, pp. 221-222), which was made a part of the religious ceremony. The chronicles are corroborated by the huacos. The Peruvian pottery graphically depicts many forms of this essentially Asiatic and ancient vice.

that "it is worthy of remark that the Egyptians, the Mexicans, and Peruvians, in their march towards civilization, should never have detected the use of iron which lay around them in abundance." [16] Prescott was mistaken as to the Egyptians and the question is not at all clear as to the Peruvians. The Iron Age in Egypt, Chaldea, Assyria, and China reaches back to 4000 B.C.[17] Iron was found in the great pyramids and a steel instrument in the tomb of Tut-ankh-Amen. In Etruria it appears as early as 1300 B.C. Mungo Park found the natives of the Niger River country, who had never seen a white man, smelting iron ore and making weapons and tools of iron.[18]

A. H. Verrill in excavations at Coclé, Panama,—in deposits he estimates as thousands of years older than the Christian era,—found "at a depth of five and one-half feet below the surface, at the temple site, among broken pottery and imbedded in charcoal . . . a steel or hardened iron implement.[19] The greater portion is almost completely destroyed by corrosion but the chisel-shaped end is in good condition. It is so hard that it is scarcely touched by a file and will scratch glass." [20] With such a tool in the hands of the great Quiché or Quichua masons, the carving of the stone columns and idols which lay about its burial place at Coclé, or even the perfectly fitted masonry blocks in the smooth walls of Cuzco, would be explained.

[16] *Conquest of Peru*, I, 126.

[17] "Iron Age," *Encyc. Brit.*, 11th ed.

[18] *Travels in the Interior of Africa*, by Mungo Park (Cassell & Co., London, 1900), Vol. II, pp. 63, 95-8.

[19] Its partial preservation is probably due to the absorbent qualities of the charcoal in which it accidentally was imbedded.

[20] "The Pompeii of Ancient America," *The World's Work*, January, 1927, p. 286.

Bourbourg [21] quotes Velasco as saying that "the Peruvians did not use iron, although they knew it under the name of *quillay,* because they knew how to temper copper like steel." [22] "*Mercurio Peruano* [23] mentions the following mines as having been worked by the Incas (or rather those who preceded them): *Escamera, Chilleo,* and *Abatanis,* gold; *Choquipiña* and *Porco,* silver; *Curahuato,* copper; *Carabuco,* lead; probably the neighborhood of *Oruro,* says Bollaert (*Antiquities,* p. 90), supplied tin; and the *magnificent iron mines* of *Ancoriames* (16° and 25′ South) on the east shore of Lake Titicaca. America is still to be discovered! It is necessary to remove the veil under which the Spanish policy has sought to cover her ancient civilization." [24]

But it seems likely that the making of steel, like letters, was a lost art when Pizarro arrived in Peru. Like the great race which worked the copper mines on Lake Michigan and built the dolmens and earthworks of the Mississippi valley, the masons of the Vilcanota were known only by their works.

[21] Int. to *Popol Vuh,* p. ccxxiv.

[22] " 'It is remarkable,' says Molina, 'that iron, which is universally supposed to have been unknown to the American natives, has a specific name in the Chilean language. It is called *panilgue* and the instruments which are made of it *chioquel,*—to distinguish them from those made of other substances, which are comprised under the generic name *nulin.*' " *The Geographical, Natural, and Civil History of Chile,* translated from the original Italian, etc., London, 1809, chap. iv.

[23] Vol. I (1791), p. 201.

[24] *Popol Vuh,* p. ccxxiv, n. 2. "Iron-working was brought into the East Indian archipelago by the megalithic immigrants. The stone-using immigrants appear to have been people well acquainted with the working of gold, copper, and iron." W. J. Perry, *Megalithic Culture of Indonesia* (Manchester, 1918), p. 178.

XXXV

WEAVING

THE Inca weavers made fine fabrics of the wool of the domestic llama and alpaca, as well as of the guanaco and vicuña which, though wild, were carefully protected by law and many of these were rounded up and shorn on great annual imperial hunts. The finest fabrics,—as fine and far more durable than silk,—were woven from the fine wool of the vicuña. This art, even after centuries of oppression and persecution, has not yet been lost by the Quichua Indians, the veritable descendants of the people over whom the Incas ruled and into whose mass the Inca caste,—or what was left of it after centuries of gradual amalgamation and the cataclysm of the conquest,—has been absorbed.

There were two varieties of indigenous cotton in Peru, produced in the Yungas or "Warm Lands" on either side of the Andes, and used in the weaving of the remarkable fabrics of the country. One of these was white, of high grade, long fiber one and one-quarter to one and one-half inches in length; the other shorter, rougher, more uneven and reddish brown in color.[1]

The so-called "Virgins of the Sun,"—eligible young girls selected, many of them, from families of Inca royal blood, and collected in convents to grow up and be edu-

[1] *The Heritage of Cotton*, by M. D. C. Crawford.
The cords found in the graves at Pachacamac and other points on the coast were made of *Agave americana*.

IRON SMELTER OF PERUVIAN INDIANS

From Historia de la Geografía del Perú, by Antonio Raimondi.

"In previous expeditions it has been recognized that the pagan Campas of Chanchamayo understood the forging of iron, but it had not been believed that they smelted it directly from the ore. It was thought that they obtained the metallic iron and prepared from it all the instruments they needed. But the discovery of a great quantity of iron ore in large chunks . . . a little distance from the smelter, and of a supply of the ore washed and ground, mixed with coal (charcoal) and ready to be smelted, furthermore the presence of slag containing bits of iron . . . removed every doubt of the fact that the so-called savages are further advanced in the iron industry than the civilized people themselves."—Raimondi, *supra*, Vol. III, p. 436.

It is possible but not likely that the Indians were taught this method of smelting iron ore by the early Spanish missionary monks.

1. Vicuña wool tapestry with cotton warps showing rare plant forms. 2. Peruvian mummy with false head and grave charms. 3. Detail of Ica embroidery show puma god with human heads. 4. Detail of fine brown cotton voile with conventional motifs. 5. Rare example of Peruvian lace. 6. Leno weave showing geometric patterns through crossing warps. 7. Ica embroidery of puma god with human sacrifices. 8. Double cloth in bird design. 9. Leno cloth in bird design with tapestry border. 10. Brocade pattern in fish convention.

From "The Heritage of Cotton," by M. B. C. Crawford. Taken from "The West Coast Leader," Lima.

cated there as religious recluses and servitors of the temple ritual,—were the most skillful weavers. This, in addition to their religious observances, was the principal part of their education. The finest fabrics, both of cotton and of wool, unsurpassed in fineness of texture, design, and finish, made for the priests and nobles and preserved in the graves of the rainless coast, were, no doubt, the work of these convents.

However, just as even to this day every Quichua woman spins,—even those we see walking with their loads along the mountain trackways,—and the children of the mountain people are still trained from infancy in the art of weaving the remarkable rugs, shawls, blankets and ponchos, characteristic of the Andes,—so in pre-Spanish times, says Crawford, "The knowledge of weaving techniques and subtleties must have been universal, since even in the coarsest webs, we find the weaver passing easily and gracefully from one technique into another in the same loom piece. In all my experience with fabrics, I have never examined any collections which showed so perfect a sense in value of texture and colour, or contain so few technical mistakes." [2]

This expert continues: "The types of fabrics in Peru include every known construction, as well as certain types impossible to produce on machine looms. I have examined and dissected tapestries, doubled cloth, brocades, warp and weft stripes, leno, dobby patterns, crocheting and laces. Besides these types of design incorporated in a fabric, they were not lacking in knowledge of the application of ornament to the finished web. They were skilled

[2] *The Heritage of Cotton, supra,* reprinted in *West Coast Leader.*

embroiderers, delighting in techniques rather more subtle than any we know of from Europe or Asia, and more closely allied to weaving. Painting, or perhaps stamping on fabrics, and even roller printing occur.

．　　　．　　　．　　　．　　　．　　　．　　　．

"In the Peruvian yarns, no matter how fine they were spun in wool or cotton, they are the absolute perfection of the spinner's art, indicating that had the wish been present, infinitely finer counts might have been spun.

．　　　．　　　．　　　．　　　．　　　．　　　．

"In one of their forms of tapestry, at each change of colour in the weft, the yarns were interlocked. This kind of weaving has no parallel that I am familiar with. They had a way, too, of outlining figures with black yarns made from human hair, and these yarns do not run at right angles as in most weaving, but in a more or less eccentric way, following the vagaries of patterns. Only an extremely skillful people could have taken such liberties with the basic principles of weaving.

"One technique I have reserved until the last. In India and Java, in the Philippine Islands, in the Gobi Desert, and in many other parts of the world through related techniques there is a process of applying design known as resist dyeing or more familiarly as *batik*. . . .

"It is very difficult to say how the discovery of such a process could have been mere accident. It demands even in its simplest form an orderly sequence of processes, which must have been thought out in advance and deliberately performed with a fixed purpose in mind. To find such a process in Peru, evidently thousands of years old, was one of the most surprising and confusing discoveries I made in my research in Peruvian fabrics." [3]

As in pottery, so in fabrics, the ancient Peruvians have left a vivid record of their customs, industry, and farm, family, and religious life. "It is the most perfect fabric-record left by any people in the history of the world. Here we do not have to rely on conjecture, traditions, or the comparisons of related arts, but may study in all their variety the actual fabrics, tools and implements, and through these safely reconstruct the processes and methods. No people in the history of fabrics, in any part of the world, have ever achieved such a high technical skill nor excelled them in a conception of design, composition, or the use of color.

"Beyond question, the most ancient specimens of cotton fabrics in all the world are those found in the desert graves of pre-Inca Peru. . . .

"It is impossible, however, to give any reliable dates for this great civilization. We can only gain some comprehension of its antiquity by a comparison with our own historic experiences.

"Roughly speaking, the people conquered by Pizarro in 1532, and known as Incas, were at about the same cultural level as our own European ancestors of the Twelfth Century. Our ancestors, indeed, excelled in the knowledge of iron and steel, but the Incas were infinitely more advanced in road and aqueduct building and in agriculture. Our ancestry had a written language but the Incas had a political and social system that had abolished those terrible famines and plagues which at times wrought such

[3] *Heritage of Cotton, supra.*

havoc in old Europe. In architecture a reasonable judge will yield the palm to South America, since our great Gothic period comes after the age I have mentioned. And so far as comforts and luxuries of life are concerned, there can be no comparison. . . .

"Our textile arts, especially as these are concerned with silk and cotton, were borrowed almost in toto from the East. Design, technique, even philology, indicate how vast is our debt to these alien peoples. Yet in spite of slow accretion of the ripening centuries of our culture, in some ways even today we have still to reach the achievements of this mysterious people of the Pacific slope of the Andes. Consequently in estimating their age, we must either attribute to them miraculous mental powers in advance of our own, or acknowledge that their civilization must have been the ripened fruit of longer periods of time than any scientist has yet dared to estimate.

. . . .

"Here is in principle the perfect miniature history of the woven web. We could reconstruct each fabric and method of construction and decoration from the evidence of these tombs. We naturally find a different emphasis in technical processes than in Asia. In a general way, the Peruvians excel in the woven design, whereas the craftsmen of India more generally emphasize the printed and dyed fabrics. But all the principal techniques occur in both areas.

. . . .

"The true explanation of the exquisite perfection of their spinning is to be sought rather in the great skill of the craftsmen themselves than in the complexity of tools

AYMARÁ LOOM

or processes. . . . Little beads of clay, metal, and wood prevented the single yarns from slipping off the spindles. These meridional beads were not of the same technical significance as the whorl placed at the bottom of the spindle, and used in northern parts of South America and Mexico.

"I have examined Peruvian single ply yarns as fine as 200's in our cotton count. . . .

"I have examined tapestries and brocades where between 200 and 300 weft yarns have been inserted to the inch in complicated patterns. Each of these designs had to be carefully calculated in advance and the least mistake would have upset the entire calculations and created a confusion in pattern. I have never seen an example of misweave in any of the finer Peruvian fabrics. . . .

"It is vain to attempt to describe the Peruvian palette of colors. Reds, purples, and different shades of blue, green, and brown predominate, but in such endless variety of tone and shade as to be impossible to limit to comparison in our modern color scheme. They belong in the same distinguished category as the colors of early Persia or of the reminiscence of the arts of Asia Minor found in the Egyptian tombs.

"The Peruvians were adept in all of the types of design which originated in the technique of weaving and their conventional forms are varied, well-balanced, and represent not only a great time in development, but a high appreciation of the sense of values in balance."

Evidently the Peruvians took the colors of their textile arts from the marvelous gamut of colors of their sky and mountains.

XXXVI

MUSIC

THOUGH not written, much of the music of the Inca people has been preserved to the present day. The principal musical instruments of the Incas were the flute and the drum. In all Inca music, both sad and gay, the predominance of these two instruments is evident. Like all Oriental music, it is based on the deep and measured rhythm of the drum-beat, caught up and merged in the plaintive wail of the flute.

Many of its notes are inexpressibly sweet. A minor cadence of sadness runs through it all, even when,—as it usually does at the close,—it quickens its time into lively action. Often the music of the Incas, or rather of the Quichua people, strikes a note of deep and unutterable despair,—the sweet memories of a lost world mingled with poignant but apparently despairing sorrow.

Nearly all Inca music gives some evidence in its regular cadence,—slow at first, continuing so, as the theme is developed, then bursting into passion of swift but controlled movement, with the same steady rhythm as its base and undertone,—of its origin in ceremonial processions and dances, and its development as an accompaniment of the various phases of their action.

Like the *Song of India,* this indigenous music of prehistoric Peru, with its basic Oriental tone, seems to give voice to the soul of a people. It nurses a sorrow as profound as the human heart; and then at times it bursts into noble aspiration. The steady rhythm of its drums was the heart-beat of the Inca people. The long refrain of its higher notes is like the sweep of the condor over the desolation of the Andes. In the measured rhythm of its lower tones one can see and hear the armed and caparisoned Incas with their disciplined followers marching on the imperial roads of the Sacred Valley.

In mourning for the dead the Incas imitated the plaintive melody of the "mourning" dove. The dove's yearning note,—repeated in unison by the populace,—was a sweet and impressive requiem.

Ultramodern music is like futurist painting.

Just as ultramodern painting, called cubist or futurist, —not that these terms mean anything, but solely because they are *different*,—harks back to primitive *abandon* but is wholly innocent of primitive sentiment and mystic significance, the latest jazz only in the same sense is fundamentally primitive. It is the drum-beat of the African negroes and the Apache Indians. Its *timbre* is the steady monotone of the savage. Like all primitive music, it is an expression of the dance and appropriately accompanies the revival of the African negro sex-dances as the sublimated essence of advanced culture.

All things move in a circle. The modern dance can be seen in its essential features around the village fires of any primitive tribe. In music and in painting, as well as in many other things, we are back at the beginning. But the Inca music, while still virile with the steady drum-beat of the march and the dance, was enveloped in a poignancy and beauty of sentiment unknown to the mere savage or to jazz.

XXXVII

LITERATURE AND FINE ARTS

WITH all of their surpassing skill in certain lines of science and mechanical arts, neither painting nor sculpture in Peru had passed the crude stages of primitive art. Flat designs in color on pottery and textiles, as well as molded forms which gave such infinite variety to Peruvian ceramics, exhibited a high order of technical skill. The figures were often grotesque, but vivid, bold, and exceedingly expressive. Sculpture in the round was confined largely to representations of idols; and these, though often of good execution, were of crude and conventional design.

Flat carving on stone, such as that of the celebrated Chavin stone, was often of mathematical perfection in balance of lines, curves and proportion, and was executed with a skill of technique never surpassed. The art of its designs, however, though long past the primitive stage of irregular and uncertain form, was as grotesque and barbarous in conception as the ultramodern "cubist" cult,—in fact there was much similarity between the two.

The songs and dramas of the Incas,—such as the play of *Apu Ollantay* (*The Great Ollantay*),[1] with its tragic plot and exquisite poetry,—were of exalted literary merit. This drama in particular, which is the only one completely

[1] Markham, *Incas*, etc., Appendix D, pp. 324-407.
Markham gives the subtitle as *A Legend of the Andes,* and says that it is of great age: Introduction to Molina, *Rites and Laws of the Yncas* (Hak. Soc.), pp. xiii-xiv.

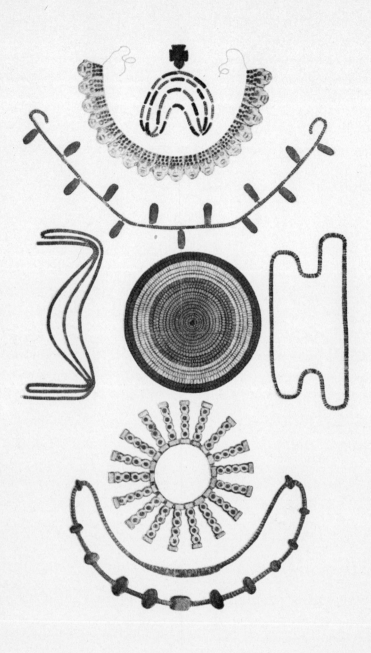

preserved, ranks in this respect with the great super-plays of other nations. This and other literary works [2] were preserved in the trained memories of the Amautas and so passed on from generation to generation.

As was the case with the literature of the Persians and Greeks, what has survived of the literature of the Incas, after the cataclysm and degradation of the conquest, is probably but a few drops of beauty from the ancient stream of Inca fancy.

In like manner folk-tales, imagined in the archaic "Golden Age" of peace and happiness by some gifted story-teller, were preserved,—like the originals of Homer's Iliad before the invention of writing,—and transmitted from age to age in the amber of exact tradition. Professional story-tellers and bards perfected and recited such tales as that of *A Famous Shepherd Named Acoyanapa, and the Beautiful and Discreet Princess, Chuquillantu, Daughter of the Sun.*[3]

These charming stories display a combination of profound knowledge of human nature with a rich imagination in the realm of the curious and strange, the marvelous and occult works of magic, characteristic of the Arabian Nights and all Oriental tales. Like the latter they are filled with a delicacy of fancy and refinement of sentiment,—a sense of dramatic values and a simplicity of expression,—which give them high rank as mere literature.[4]

[2] Such as the play *Anaysauca* (How Pleasant!); *Hayacucho*, etc. Markham, Introduction to Molina, *Rites and Laws of the Yncas* (Hak. Soc.), p. xiv.

[3] Markham, *Incas of Peru*, Appendix E, pp. 408-414.

[4] "'The Amautas composed both tragedies and comedies, which were represented before the Inca and his court on solemn occasions. The subject matter of the tragedy related to military deeds and the victories of former times; while the arguments of the comedies were on agricultural and fa-

The Prayers and Hymns of the Incas were comparable to the Songs of David and the Invocations of Job.

Europe of the Renaissance, which had carried letters forward from the art of mere writing to the art of printing, was immeasurably superior in fine arts, architecture, general enterprise and learning to the Incas, although it was inferior to them in the general comfort of the people and in some industrial arts, such as weaving and agriculture.

Even Europe of the twelfth century, which has been compared by some writers with the stage of culture of Mexico and Peru at the time of the Conquest, had the immeasurable advantage of its documentary articulate written records as an incentive and aid to thought. Tradition,

---

miliar household subjects. They understood the composition of long and short verses, with the right number of syllables in each. . . .' Salcamayhua also bears witness to the existence of the ancient drama, and gives the names for four different kinds of plays called *Anay Sauca*, a joyous representation, *Hayachuca, Llama-llama*, a farce, and *Hanamsi*, a tragedy." Sir Clements Markham, *Incas of Peru*, p. 147. His quotation is from Garcilasso de la Vega.

Sir Clements Markham gives a charming account of his trip over the cordillera of the Paucartambo to the house of "the old cura" of Laris, Dr. Pablo Justiniani. From him Markham obtained permission to copy his manuscripts of "old Quichua songs" and *Ollantay*. "It was necessary to cross the lofty range of mountains which bounds the lovely vale of the Vilcamayu, to pass over grassy plateaux at a great elevation, where the sapphire blue of the small alpine lakes contrasted with the dark surfaces of the precipitous cliffs, and then to descend, by winding paths, into the secluded vale of Laris. Here there was a small church, a few huts, and a house consisting of buildings on two sides of a courtyard, with the church tower seen over the roof. Away in one direction there was a wooded glen of great depth, containing one small house built over a spring . . . A small stream flowed down another ravine of wonderful beauty, with lofty mountains on either side."

Here Markham enjoyed his conversations with the descendant of the Incas. "In the intervals of copying manuscripts" he "took long rambles down the beautiful vale of Yanatilde, and rejoiced to see the friendly relations that existed between the old cura and his parishioners, who raised crops of potatoes and ocas, and kept flocks of llamas which found pasturage on the mountain slopes."—Markham, *Incas of Peru*, pp. 144-46.

highly developed by trained historians, as it was in Peru, —even though aided by the quipus (records kept by knotted cords of various strands and colors and read with remarkable skill by trained professional interpreters called Quipucamayocs),—could not supply the place of writing.[5]

It was from written documents that learning was revived in Europe in the great uplift of human intelligence and endeavor of which the discovery of the new world and the conquest of Peru itself were incidents.   There was no such uplift in the Inca culture at that time and could not be without a better means than mere tradition and oral teaching for the accumulation and enlargement of human knowledge.   Such uplift as that culture had

[5] Montesinos reports the tradition that in the chaos and "dark ages" which followed the overthrow of Pachacuti VI in the Battle Gap of Vilcanota, by the hordes from the south, "writing was lost." It is established by the well-authenticated traditions collected by Sarmiento and also by Garcilasso's history that events were recorded by pictures on boards. No doubt the pictures on the wooden vases still preserved in all the vividness of their excellent coloring in the museum of Cuzco are records of historic events. The manuscript of Huaman Poma makes it "almost certain that portraits of the Incas and their queens once existed." (Markham, *Incas*, etc., p. 141.)

A crude portrait of one of the Incas is still to be seen perfectly preserved, with strong Caucasian features, painted in red on the cliff above Ollantaytambo. It was possibly from the same sources from which Huaman Poma made his pen and ink sketches of the Incas and obtained his description of the color of the tunic and vestment of each Inca that Doctor Justo Sahuaraura, lineal descendant in the seventh generation from Huayna Ccapac, obtained the remarkable series of portraits of the Incas from Ayar Manco to Tupac Amaru, which he published in his *Monarquia Peruana*.

The engraved wooden boards found in Easter Island (referred to above and fully described in the *Journal of the Polynesian Society*) tend to corroborate not only the tradition of picture-writing in Peru but also the hypothesis of communication between that country and Easter Island.

As a matter of fact the conventional figures and lines of figures of the sacred serpent and falcon engraved on the walls of Chan-Chan, and the falcon-headed god (the same as in Asia and Egypt), repeated over and over as by way of an overwhelming appeal, making obeisance to the central figure of the Creator on the monolithic gate of Tiahuanaco, vividly represent a certain stage of picture-writing.

in the great megalithic age,—the epoch of the great navigators of Polynesia, and of the discovery and settlement of America by way of the Pacific,—had subsided. Its culture had flowered, borne its fruit, and decayed before the European Renaissance had brought Columbus and Pizarro to America.

The great white *Ayar* or *Arya* race from whom the Incas were descended, which had produced the marvelous megalithic culture of Peru, had largely disappeared, as it had in Asia, by the slow but steady process of amalgamation with the mass of darker indigenous people.

The very presence of the Spaniards in Peru,—the ships in which they had come, the equipment they brought,—showed their superiority in knowledge, spirit, enterprise, and power to the Incas of that age.[6]

[6] The work of the ancient Peruvians in gold, silver, and precious stones was exquisite. The modern Quichuas have inherited much of this artistic taste and technical skill. Even now the modern Indians make representations of birds and other objects of nature or fancy in spun gold filigree which cannot be surpassed.

MAP OF COLONIAL PERU

From Historia de la Geografía del Peru, by Antonio Raimondi.

The continuous lines indicate the Inca roads; the broken lines indicate probable Inca roads of which the data is not certain. New Castile (Nueva Castilla), so named by the Spanish Government of the "Indies" as the jurisdiction allotted to Pizarro in the quarrel between him and Almagro, includes the greater part of what is now the Republics of Ecuador and Perú. New Toledo (Nueva Toledo), covered by the southern part of the map, is the northern portion of the jurisdiction so named given to Almagro. His province extended further south and included also what is now Chile and a good part of Argentina. The portion of New Toledo appearing on the map was called in Colonial times Upper Perú. It is now the Republic of Bolivia, and a portion of southern Peru.

The Inca Empire included the entire area covered by the map north and south, and more,—as it extended further south and took in what is now Tucuman in northern Argentina, and also the greater part of Chile.

East and west the Inca Empire reached from the coast across the Andes and a considerable distance into the timbered country of the Yungas or low "hot lands" on the upper waters of the tributaries of the Amazon inhabited by the *Antis,*—wild, uncivilized tribes of Indians, mostly enemies of the so-called Quichua-Ayamará population ruled by the Incas. This last region was the Anti-Suyu, or eastern realm of the four realms into which the Empire was divided, and to which the four roads led from Cuzco.

It will be noticed on Raimondi's map that a road extended from Calca on the upper Vilcanota across the cordillera by way of Paucartambo to Pilcopata on the headwaters of the Madre de Dios; and that there was probably a road connecting this toward the south with another road which left Ayavirí and crossed the central Andes above the head of Lake Titicaca by way of Sandia and extended far into the Yungas along a tributary of the Beni by way of San Juan del Oro. In this section there are said to be vast beds of gold-bearing gravel, and it is thought that the Incas obtained a great part of their store of gold from the placers in this region. The immense golden slab forming the image of the Sun in the temple at Cuzco has never yet been found by the Spanish conquerors.

The splendid stone stairway by which the ancient highway mounted the heights of Pisac en route to Paucartambo and beyond, is still in place and still in use. A graded road, paved in places, passed further to the north down the Vilcanota river below Ollantaytambo than is indicated on Raimondi's map. Its level reaches along the great walls of the agricultural terraces and the massive parapets of the megalithic fortress of Salapunco are still in use and in good condition,—still drained by the ancient underground stone conduits.

In the north it will be noticed that a road extended across the mountains east from Quito, the northern capital of the Incas, into the Montaña, to the forks of the Napo. From the Chimu capital of Chan-Chan (near the Spanish Colonial city of Trujillo,—marked Truxillo on Raimondi's map) a road, going north and east, is indicated as far east as Moyobamba by way of Cajamarca and Chachapoyas. This road, however, extended still further east, to Lamas and Tarapoto in the beautiful valley of the lower Mayo river.

There was also a road, not indicated on the map, extending far to the south of La Paz along the great inter-cordilleran pampa.

The great naturalist and geographer, Raimondi, walked over a great portion of Perú, measured distances, studied the resources of the country and made a careful survey on which his map is based.

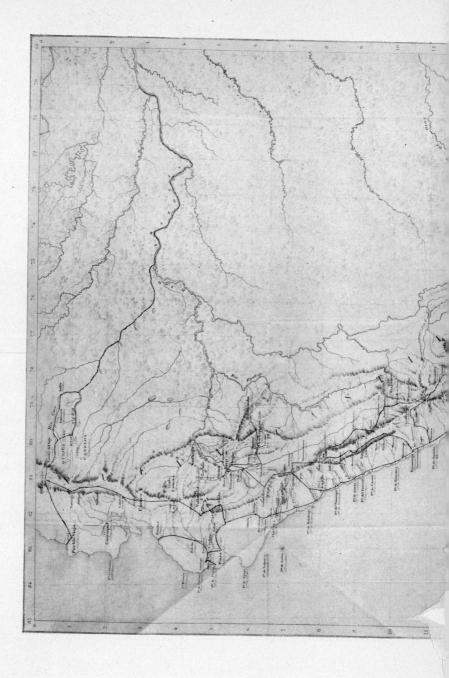

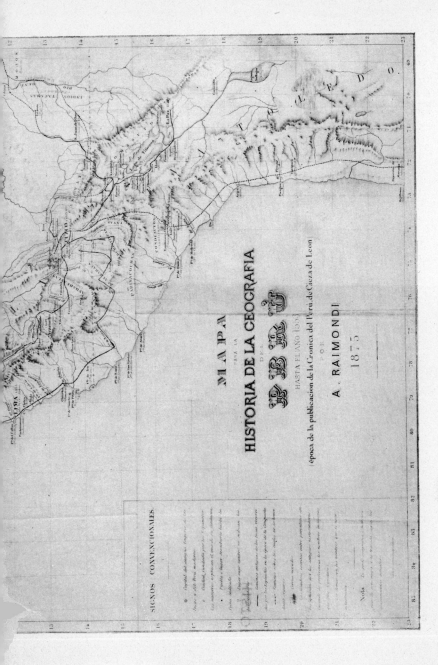

MAPA
PARA LA
HISTORIA DE LA GEOGRAFIA
DEL
PERU
HASTA EL AÑO 1553
(época de la publicacion de la Cronica del Perú de Cieza de Leon)
POR
A. RAIMONDI
1875

SIGNOS CONVENCIONALES.

XXXVIII

ROADS

ONE of the most important factors in the economic, social, and political organization and control of the Inca state was its system of communication. Some of the descriptions of the Inca roads, creating the impression that they were paved and well-graded highways leading in all cardinal directions throughout the empire, are misleading. The Incas had no wheeled vehicles and the roads were intended only for foot passengers and the llama,—which then, as now, was used as a beast of burden.

Even the celebrated imperial highway from Quito to Cuzco descended and ascended the deep gorges of the rivers by steep grades, with stone steps or stairways in places,—crossing the swift mountain streams on suspension bridges supported by cables made of withes, woven fibers, and forest lianas. Where the way led along the pampa or on easy grades of the slopes or quebradas it was merely a trackway worn by the travelers. At places in the Vilcanota Valley and elsewhere in the Andes, where the thoroughfares of the Incas crossed marshy or uneven ground, the highway was walled, graded, drained, and splendidly paved with unerring engineering skill.

A parallel north and south road on the coast where it crossed the sandy wastes of the desert, was merely marked by lines of posts and, in the irrigated valleys, enclosed in parallel adobe fences or walls, fixing the line of passage like our modern country lanes or narrow alleys in the towns.

There were tambos,—rest houses and storehouses of supplies,—at convenient distances along the highway; and swift runners, relayed at frequent intervals, carried the commands of the government, the messages and business of those who were able to command their services, with remarkable celerity between the communities of the immense empire.

ANCIENT STONE-PAVED ROADWAY, VILCANOTA
VALLEY

Photograph by the author.

BRIDGE AT OLLANTAYTAMBO

The pier in the middle of the river is a prehistoric structure. The size of the stones can be estimated by comparison with the people standing on them. Note the abandoned terraces on the steep hillside in the background. A bridge swung in a similar manner as the present structure, on the same piers now in place, has been in use here since prehistoric times.

XXXIX

AGRICULTURE AND STOCK-BREEDING

In agriculture the Peruvians had developed the cultivation of as many as sixty-five native plants. Some of these, such as the potato and the tomato, they had developed from comparatively worthless wild originals to the delicious vegetables which we owe today to the skill and persistence of the Quichua farmers. The potato had become the basic food supply of the Inca empire, surpassing in value even corn (maize) which was also an important food plant of the Peruvians, brought, probably, originally from Mexico in the trade of the peoples along the coast, north and south, in archaic primitive times.[1]

The delicious Lima bean is another gift to us of the Inca farmers. Many other beans; oca, a valuable root crop resembling the potato; quinoa, a grain which ripens at 12,000 feet in the Andes, are in the long list of the Inca food plants cultivated with matchless skill in the enriched and irrigated terrace gardens.

How much, if any, of this food-plant culture had been developed by Quichua or Aymará tribes in the Andes, the Yungas Indians on the coast, or the ancestors of these people, before the arrival of the Ayar leaders (ancestors of the Inca ruling caste) cannot now be said. The breeding of species of corn and potatoes which will grow and

[1] The value to the world of the potato, which was first cultivated and developed in the Peruvian Andes, has been mentioned elsewhere in the author's works on Peru.

255

mature at altitudes respectively of 12,500 and 14,500 feet, must have required many centuries of effort. Descendants of these same Quichua and Aymará farmers still produce a small-eared corn about the shores of Lake Titicaca and large crops of potatoes on the slopes around Lake Junin.

At any rate the culture of these food plants was no doubt improved and extended by the art of the new rulers. It is very probable that even before the arrival of the white megalithic "builders and civilizers," the indigenous people had tamed the guanaco and the vicuña and had bred from them the llama and alpaca. This achievement is undoubtedly one of the most interesting and useful events in the world's history of live-stock culture. It was probably carried forward to greater excellence and extent under the rule of the Ayar-Incas.

The alpaca especially, with its immense fleece of long wool, is a tribute to the patience and skill of the ancient Andean breeders. This curious animal, which is more like a large long-necked and long-legged sheep than its cousin, the "Camel of the Andes," requires extraneous aid in the act of procreation.

"PACHACUTIC INCA"

Father of the Conqueror Tupac Yupanqui. Grandfather of the Imperial Inca Huayna Ccapac. Great-Grandfather of Atahualpa who was executed by Pizarro.

Ninety-ninth Ayar king in line from Pirua Paccari Manco in the Blas Valera list. "The greatest man that the American race has ever produced." (Sir Clements R. Markham.)

"The Prince Cusi was the builder of the empire, the foundations of which were laid by Rocca. The elaborate religious ceremonial, the methods of recording events, the military organization, the self-working social system were his work. It may seem incredible that the whole fabric of Andean civilisation should be the work of one man, and it would be if he had created it. But Cusi was not the creator. He was the Pachacuti, the reformer. Over all the regions that he conquered there were the same ideas and habits of thought, and of living, dialects of the same original language, and the same faint memories of an almost forgotten past. Pachacuti worked upon these materials with the skill and foresight of a profound statesman. His grand object was attained, for he welded together a homogeneous empire with such masterly thoroughness in all its complicated details that its machinery worked almost automatically."

He finished, as he had lived, in style.

After reigning for one hundred and three years (Sarmiento, Hak. Soc., p. 139), as his end approached: "He had his sons and his councillors around him. Addressing Tupac, he said (SIR CLEMENTS R. MARKHAM, *The Incas of Peru*, pp. 91, 93): 'My son, you know how many great nations I leave to you, and you know what labour they have cost me. Mind that you are the man to keep and augment them.' He made his other sons plough furrows and he gave them weapons, in token that they were to serve and to fight for their sovereign. He turned to Tupac, saying, 'Care for them, and they will serve you.' He expressed some wishes about his obsequies, ordering that his body should be placed in his palace of Pata-llacta. Then he began to croon in a low and sad voice:

> " 'I was born as a flower of the field,
> As a flower I was cherished in my youth.
> I came to my full age, I grew old;
> Now I am withered and die.'

He told those around him that he went to rest with his father the sun—and so he departed."

"PACHACUTIC INCA"

*From "Monarquia Peruana," by Dr. Justo
Sahuaraura, Inca.*

(See reverse side for description)

XL

VALUATION OF INCA CULTURE

THERE is much difference of opinion as to the merit of the Inca culture. There is no doubt it was in a state of decline at the time of the advent of Pizarro. It is true that the old line of the Ayars, whose ancestors, in far prehistoric times, had constructed the megalithic works and which had been in eclipse for many centuries, had been restored some five centuries before the arrival of the Spaniards. But the purity of the ancient religion, as well as of the race itself, had been degraded. Idols and fetishes and magic had largely supplanted the worship of Viracocha.

The Inca rule had reached its greatest extent in the reign of the grandfather of Atahualpa who was captured and executed by Pizarro; but even as to this, disintegration had begun. Huayna Ccapac had transferred for a time his seat of government from Cuzco, the ancient capital, to Quito, and jealousies had arisen between the north and south. War broke out between Atahualpa, coming from Quito, and his brother Huascar, reigning at Cuzco. Huascar had just been defeated by one of Atahualpa's generals when the Spanish adventurers arrived at Cajamarca.

The value to be placed on the Inca culture, or "civilization," depends on the standards which are to govern. If it is to be measured by its military power, its ability to "take its own part," to withstand attack, it probably never stood high in comparison with European powers, and certainly in this respect at the time of Pizarro's arrival it was contemptible.

Perhaps we should be slow to judge an ancient civilization, such as the Inca or the Chinese, by the standards of war. Mr. Massingham has written a great book (*Downland Man*) to prove by the story of the same archaic civilization in England that the advent of the standard of war was a plunge of the human race from light to darkness; and of course, as to the mere choice and effect as between war and peace, he is right.

But nevertheless the downfall of the megalithic culture of England, whose beautiful spirit he depicts, as well as that of the kindred and equally refined and beautiful culture of the Ayar-Incas of Peru, was due to the utter inability to make war in self-defense. Both were overthrown in a contemptible struggle by a miserable handful of invaders.

In fact one point of similarity and identity of the megalithic cultures of England and Peru was that both were essentially and entirely cultures of peace. This was both their strength and their weakness. It enabled them to organize a unified and disciplined industrial state by which alone the culture of their marvelous arts, the apparent contentment and well-being of even the masses of their people, and the construction of stoneworks and earthworks, which impress one as the works of supermen, was made possible. At the same time this inability to make war, even in self-defense when attacked, led to the destruction of both.

This decay of the archaic civilization as pictured by Massingham and attributed by him to the advent of the war spirit, was as much due in Peru to the growth of immoral and degenerate practices and the falling away from the "old religion." This was constantly denounced and bemoaned by the great Inca leaders and Amautas (Wise Men),—just as in the exactly parallel case the apostasy and degeneracy of the old Jews was denounced by Moses and the Prophets. In both cases the disasters which fell upon the peoples were attributed to their disobedience of the "law" and the worship of "false gods."

When the descendants of the Ayars at Cuzco had again fallen into vice, an ambitious lady, Siu Yacu (spelled by Montesinos *Ciuaco*), said to have been of the blood royal, led the revolution which reestablished the ancient discipline. Her instrument was her son Rocca.

Rocca, when he assumed the leadership, reprobated, as his mother had done, the falling away from the old religion. "No one can doubt," he said to the people, "the special love which my father the sun feels for us. When he weakened the power of the realm so that it fell to pieces, he took care to provide a remedy. It was vice and sloth which consumed its grandeur, and reduced it almost to a vanishing point. . . . Now his providence will apply a remedy. His command is that you must obey me in all things, as his son. My first decree is that you must apply yourselves to warlike exercises . . . for it was by discipline and exercises that our ancestors became Lords of the World, as our *Quipucamayocs* tell us." [1]

The growth of magic and the degradation of the gods,

---

[1] *The Incas of Peru*, by Sir Clements R. Markham, pp. 62-63. The strategy employed by Siu Yacu and her sorceress sister to impress the people with the divine mission of *Rocca* was dramatic and magnificent. Markham, *supra*, pp. 60-62.

like the "Fall of Lucifer" in archaic England, which Massingham speaks of so eloquently in his great work, was a consequence, in fact part and parcel, of this degeneracy. The breaking up of the habits of peaceful industry by which the colossal works of the megalithic age in Peru and England had been made possible,—prehistoric invasions, the substitution of fear for reverence as the dominant motive of men's lives,—is as graphically recorded in the traditions and monuments of the Incas as Massingham pictures them in the overthrow and decay of the civilization of the barrow-builders, miners, and farmers of "megalithic" England.[2]

[2] The graphic picture which Massingham draws of the "Divine Lords," "Children of the Sun,"—whose immortal tombs are the "long-barrows" crowning the high-places of the Downlands,—is rather inconsistent with his apparent assumption that this Downland Megalithic society was a democratic one of a homogeneous race of "small dark-skinned" people, descended from the Egyptians.

Such stupendous works as the colossal terraces and earthworks of England, just as the pyramids of Egypt, the Cyclopean walls of the Caroline Islands, and the megalithic masonry of Peru, could only have been possible in a society of enslaved labor or a socialistic state, which was the equivalent of slavery, ruled over by a higher caste of just such "Divine Lords" as sleep in the colossal tombs of the pyramids and the long-barrows.

As yet no colored race has displayed the energy of such leadership nor the exalted conception of such works.

The *labor* was no doubt performed by a colored and enslaved, or practically enslaved, population under the command of *white* rulers of a dominant race, who held the docile obedience of the masses of an inferior people by inculcating them with the conception that the ruling lords were divine "Children of the Sun," or of the reigning god. This idea has come down almost to our own time and among our own kinsmen in the doctrine of the "Divine Right of Kings."

In fact, it is very likely that the decline and final degeneracy of the "Downland Man," as pictured by Massingham, like that of the culture of the ancient Jews, the Egyptians, the Hindu-Aryans, the Ayar-Incas, and the Toltecs, was due as much to the corruption of the blood of the white ruling race and its gradual absorption and final disappearance in the mass of the dark indigenous people as to anything else.

However, even at the time of the conquest many traces of the old superior race were left in the Inca caste. Markham, *Incas of Peru*, p. 121.

In the ancient Quichua-Inca language, the same word, *aucca*, signified *enemy* and *warrior;* so that at least in primitive times the Incas' conception of a warrior was apparently only as an enemy. The white Ayar gained his ascendancy over his followers and over the darker indigenous people of Peru by the arts of peace rather than war.

He came with the doctrine of peace and brotherly love, as proven by the oldest traditions of the people. He taught the nomad shepherds and hunters to till the ground, to irrigate the desert, to build megalithic works of masonry which have never been surpassed. He taught them the marvelous art of weaving, which they carried to a degree of mechanical perfection and artistic taste and judgment which is said by competent judges never to have been equaled by any other people.[3]

But above all this the archaic Ayar leaders taught the indigenous people of an unseen omnipotent spirit God,—Viracocha,—the Creator and Ruler of the world. The Inca told the native people that he was himself the son of Viracocha. In this, as in many other features of his culture, the Inca showed himself to be religiously related to our own race,—as we also worship God as "Our Father."

At the same time he worshipped the sun as the great son of Viracocha, Illuminator of the World,—more understandable to the common people. He constructed the magnificent ritual of sun-worship and erected temples of stone dedicated to the great solar deity in the "high-places" of the Andes. Magnificent as is the apparition of this great celestial luminary everywhere,—nowhere in

[3] M. D. C. Crawford, *The Heritage of Cotton*, New York, 1924.

the world is the cult of his deification and worship more appealing than in the bleak heights of the Andes as he rises and sets among the cordilleras in indescribable glory.

The indigenous and familiar religion of the people was also of distinct Oriental origin,—the worship of the ancestor of the *Ayllu*, family, or clan; and as the old religion became debased innumerable fetishes and totems arose.

With this doctrine of divine descent of the Inca and the royal caste, it was easy for the Ayar leaders, priests, and statesmen, to establish the socialistic state,—the basis of the Peruvian political system,—ruled over by the Inca himself as an absolute monarch, aided by a council of state and high officials of royal blood. In this royal caste the women, many of whom displayed great ability, often exerted powerful influence. This is especially shown by the traditions of the leading part taken by Mama Ocllo, the "august princess"; Huaco, the "warlike princess"; and the other sister-wives of the Ayar chiefs in their migration from Paccari-Tampu.[4]

As a sample of shrewd Inca diplomacy, even down to within a century and a half of the Spanish conquest, the following passage describes the manner in which several rich coast valleys were brought under the religion and domain of the Inca empire.

"In the year 1374 the two Incas made a voyage to the valleys of Pachacamac, Rimac, Chancay, and Huaman (today Barranco), subject to the great *Cuis Mancu* who ruled as King. To the demands of the Incas, *Cuis Mancu* replied that he had for his gods, *Pachaca-*

[4] Markham, *supra*, p. 49 *et seq.*

mac, the supreme god and creator of the universe; the idol, *Rimac;* the vixen, by reason of its cunning; *Mama Cocha* (the sea) from whom they took their sustenance; and that he was prepared to fight and defend himself. The Incas approached him with the purpose of overcoming him by argument. *Cuis Mancu* sallied out with an armed troop. *Ccapac Upanqui* sent to him proposing that they should agree to an armistice until the one side and the other should have their say [*se ventilase*] about their gods; and that they (the Incas) would permit the worship of the god, *Rimac,* to the same extent that *Cuis Mancu* and his people should agree to worship the *Sun,* to which they added other arguments.

"The King, *Cuis Mancu,* and his Council, having heard the proposal, agreed to a truce and the parties conferred for many days. Finally peace was concluded on the following conditions:

"First. That the Incas should worship the Sun;

"Second. That a temple should be erected to Pachacamac and sacrifices should be made to him, but not of human blood;

"Third. That the idols should be cast out of the temple of Pachacamac;

"Fourth. That a house of the Chosen Virgins of the Sun should be founded in that valley;

"Fifth. That the King, *Cuis Mancu,* should continue in the government of his dominions, recognizing at the same time as his Supreme Lord, the Inca of Cuzco, and should obey the Incas' laws;

"Sixth. That the Incas should hold in veneration the idol Rimac.

"Peace having been agreed to upon these terms and the necessary garrison having been established, they returned to Cuzco in 1376, the King, *Cuis Mancu*, accompanying them to the capital." [5]

Note the patience with which the Incas proceeded. They were occupied for two years on this mission. Certainly this contrasts favorably with much of the diplomacy and much of the missionary effort of our own times and our own country.

From a standpoint of industrial efficiency within the limits of their culture, the state machine, organized and directed by the Incas, has never been surpassed. It was only by some such concentration of the full power of the state that the walled terraces of the "hanging" gardens; the huge systems of irrigation; the stone cities, temples, and palaces of the Vilcanota and other valleys of the Andes, or the great brick and adobe structures on the coast of Peru could have been constructed.

Likewise it was only by such a coordinated employment of the entire population and the controlled specialization in art and industry made possible by it, that the Inca state, cut off as it was from frequent communication with other continents, was able to develop the arts,— whose principles their ancestors had brought from Asia,— along original lines to such perfection as was attained in the most skillful intensified agriculture; the breeding and domestication of plants and animals; the masonry in stone never elsewhere surpassed; the working of gold, silver,

[5] *Kon, Pachacamac, Uirakocha;* by Luis E. Valcarcel (University of Cuzco, 1912), pp. 21-22.

tin, copper, and possibly (in very ancient times) iron; the weaving of fabrics in cotton and wool which in fineness of texture, in animation, originality, and taste of color and design, as well as in perfection of technique, have not been rivaled in any other land,—and especially have not been equaled in our own machine age.

There are evidences of the surgical skill of the Incas in the number of trepanned skulls which have been found in the graves.[6]

[6] "The aborigines possessed advanced medical knowledge making use of a magnificent flora, full today of secrets to us. They knew how to reduce luxation effectively and employed fixation to consolidate fractures, sometimes having recourse in both cases to kneading (massage); they knew the dangers of free exposure of wounds to the air, curing these very thoroughly; they could easily distinguish syphilis, rheumatism, agues, fevers, cerebral disturbances, mental aberration, etc.

"Fragments of flint sharpened to a point were used for bleeding and excising pterygiums, and the same sharpened on the edge for cutting the umbilical cord.

"Lastly they possessed a perfect process of mummification. It does not seem strange, therefore, surgical science being so advanced in prehistoric Peru, that on the presentation of a broken skull they should attempt ways to extract the fragments of bone, to raise and draw out successively the sunken plates, to adjust the points and in a word with their primitive instruments, as primitive as those of ancient Greece and Persia, to accomplish the linear readjustment of the edges of the fracture forming a quadrangular or polygonal orifice."

M. A. Muñiz, M.D., in *Report* of U.S. Bureau of Ethnology, 1894-95, p. 11.

XLI

A CONTEMPTIBLE STRUGGLE

A flash of anger and their empire sank
Deep down in the unfathomable deep;
One draught of all their hopes and dreams she drank,
And then she went to sleep.

J. Macmillan Brown, *The Riddle of the Pacific.*

The Incas went down finally and forever in a feeble and contemptible defense of their empire.

Though great emperors had arisen and carried on campaigns for the extension of their domain, the opposition they had overcome was but feeble. Though at the height of their so-called power (judged at least by the geographical extent of their empire) when Pizarro arrived, the whole structure of the Peruvian state fell like a card house without a single effective blow struck in its defense.

It was an empire of ten million people. Pizarro's force consisted of 168 men, of whom sixty-two were cavalry. Three had firearms (arquebuses). Pizarro's men were protected by mail and a "few" (not over twenty) were armed with crossbows.[1]

On the coast there was no fighting at all. It was a strange drama of self-assertion on the part of Pizarro and supreme obedience on the part of the people. Probably they accepted him as a second Inca. He at once proceeded to parcel out the land *and the people* among his

[1] Prescott, *Conquest of Peru*, I, 269-70.

266

followers. There does not seem even to have been an objection made.

The Inca nation as judged by its conduct at the time of its downfall was a degenerate slave state and a change of rulers apparently made little difference to the people. In what Prescott describes as a fight at Cajamarca after Pizarro had penetrated into the mountains, where the Inca, accompanied by an army of Quichua veterans, was resting, not a single Spanish soldier was killed and the only wound which any Spaniard received was a slight cut on the wrist received by Pizarro himself as he raised his arm to defend Atahualpa from the attack of some of Pizarro's own men who sought to kill the Inca whom Pizarro wished to save.[2]

Prescott estimates that the Spaniards on this occasion slaughtered somewhere between two thousand and ten thousand of the Inca's followers, fixing the approximate number at six thousand, the mean between the two thousand given by Pizarro's secretary on the one hand, and the ten thousand given by Garcilasso on the other.[3] Prescott says that the fighting lasted about thirty minutes. Even at the lowest figure given of the number of slain, the Spaniards must have been kept quite busy, as, according to this, on the average, each individual Spaniard killed a dozen of the Inca's followers in thirty minutes.[4]

No doubt the Peruvians were confused and startled by

[2] *Ibid.*, p. 306.
[3] *Ibid.*, p. 307.
[4] A similar absurd exaggeration seems quite apparent in the report cited by Prescott (Vol. I, p. 276) that the Inca's army at this time numbered 50,000 men and in that distinguished author's statement that five thousand or six thousand of the Inca's followers had entered the plaza of Cajamarca when the attack was launched upon them by Pizarro and his band of 168.

the strange sight of the horses,—the centaur men; and by the noise and effect of the few firearms. It may have seemed to them like the thunder of Viracocha, the old Jehovah, lord of the lightning and the sky. This was especially so as these strange men who carried the thunder,—some of them mounted on strange animals,—were white, and the tradition was that Viracocha, who had once appeared as a white man, would once more come among them.

But the Inca-Quichuas were not a savage race of fighters like the warrior Iroquois, merely overcome and terror-stricken at first by the thunder and flash of the firearms of Champlain. They were a civilized race led by a great emperor,—descendant of a long line of emperors and wise men. With all allowance for the first surprise and shock of fear, and the superstitious dread of the white Viracochas, had they been a real fighting race, like the unconquered Araucanians of Chile, or the Iroquois or Sioux, they would soon have recovered themselves and overwhelmed the handful of audacious strangers who had desecrated their Inca.

Even after Atahualpa had been captured at Cajamarca, it would have been a simple matter for his followers to surround Pizarro and his men and to prevent their escape from the town. But there was no fight in them. They were mere automatons and slaves. An empire, rich in gathered gold, but immeasurably richer in the fabulous silver mines soon discovered in its mountain peaks, and richer yet than these in the slave labor of its people, fell without a real blow. Never was a prize so rich or so rotten ripe for the plucking as that which fell upon his touch into the daring hand of Pizarro.[5]

The capture and execution of Atahualpa determined the fate of the Inca empire. There was some desultory fight-

[5] The drama of Pizarro's stroke at Cajamarca has been too well described by Prescott and others to require repetition.

The audacity of Pizarro at the head of his small band of adventurers amid the unknown dangers of the New World was even more remarkable than that of his cousin Cortes in Mexico. For intensity of color and action the scene is not surpassed in all the annals of the marvelous in man's career. The perfidy of the ruse (well described by Prescott) by which the Spaniards secured possession of the person of Atahualpa was only equaled by the Inca's inexplicable apathy and trust in putting himself at the mercy of the ruthless strangers. Once in Pizarro's possession there was as little hope of justice for him as there was for Charles I or the late Czar Nicholas.

Atahualpa yielded to Pizarro's request that he should meet the Spanish commander with an unarmed escort. As the Inca entered the stone-built city where in his courteous hospitality he had assigned quarters to Pizarro and his troop,—at the sound of a bugle the Spaniards fell upon him, sword and arquebus, killed his attendants and took the Inca prisoner.

One can yet visit in the ancient village of Cajamarca, set in its pleasant mid-zone pampa, the "*Rescate*" (ransom),—the room which Atahualpa filled with gold under his agreement with Pizarro that at such a price he would be set free. The matchless Quichua masonry, with its classic idol-niches in the wall, still stands intact.

As the golden booty reached the line on the wall,—the height which a man could reach, which had been agreed upon as the measure of the Inca's ransom,—the greedy Spaniards, as they feasted their eyes upon the golden hoard, could wait no longer for a division of the spoils. They declared the ransom agreement fulfilled and the Inca's messengers stopped the delivery of the gold. Pizarro was eager to proceed to Cuzco and seize the remainder of the treasure before it could be concealed. Prescott estimated the gold delivered by Atahualpa as the equivalent of fifteen and a half million dollars in the money of that author's time (1846). Its equivalent in present day values would be much more.

In the interval before Pizarro arrived at the imperial capital the golden statue of the conqueror Tupac Yupanqui (grandfather of Atahualpa), the great golden image of the sun, and the rest of the golden treasure of the Incas was hidden. It has never been discovered. The secret of its hiding-place was lost with the death of its sole possessor. Despondent over the failure of an attempted uprising of his oppressed people and despairing of his country, the last keeper of the secret died without communicating it to anyone.

(Sir Clements R. Markham talked with a lady in Cuzco who was present when the leader of the abortive insurrection returned to her house with his golden burden,—a portion of the treasure which the keeper had given him

ing afterwards, and at Cuzco a few of the Inca chiefs gave a better account of themselves. But it was entirely futile. A few hundred skillful bowmen stationed in the mountain passes could easily have destroyed both men and horses of the small Spanish squadron, while remaining themselves in perfect safety. For some strange reason, although well acquainted with the use of the bow,—from which in the past they had suffered disaster,—the Incas, in what little fighting they did, relied upon hand-to-hand combat, in which the Spaniards had the advantage.

On the very entrance of Pizarro into Cuzco the people of the socialistic monarchy were ready to accept and even acclaim the new ruler. "The only sounds that disturbed the repose of the Spaniards were the noises of feasting

to pay the expenses of the movement for freedom. He had been taken blindfolded up the bed of the Huatanay rivulet at Cuzco in the night and into the hidden treasury. The covering was removed from his eyes and "he suddenly found himself surrounded by vases, cups, plates, ingots, and great statues, all of pure gold, in incredible profusion." *Incas of Peru*, p. 288.)

In the state museum in Lima there is an excellent painting in which the high lights of the scene of Atahualpa's execution by Pizarro are well depicted,—the arrogance of the Spanish conqueror, the anguish of the Inca's wives, the horror and perplexity of the Inca's attendants at the sight of the sacrilege of the violation of his sacred person, the smug sanctimoniousness of the priest, Valverde, as he offered the unfortunate imperial descendant of an immemorial line of kings, as a bribe for his acceptance of the faith of a merciful Christ, the consolation of being strangled instead of being burned alive.

The Inca accepted the proposal and was garroted.

Atahualpa left one son and two daughters. The son was baptized by the Spanish priests Francisco Atahualpa. One of the daughters, baptized Angelina, had an illegitimate son by Francisco Pizarro. This boy was baptized in his father's name, Francisco Pizarro. Francisco Pizarro (the conqueror) also had an illegitimate daughter by Doña Inez Huayllar Ñusta, a daughter of Huayna Ccapac. The child was baptized Francisca Pizarro. She grew up in Lima but later went to Spain and married her uncle, Hernando Pizarro, while he was held there in prison. After the latter's death she returned to Lima and married Martin Ampuero of that city,—"whence comes the house of Ampuero." (Dr. Justo Sahuaraura, *Monarquia Peruana*, p. 39.)

and dancing, which the natives, with happy insensibility, constantly prolonged to a late hour of the night." [6]

If the people had known of the misery that was to follow, their attitude probably would have been different. But even then it is doubtful if there would have been a different result. They had been too long without initiative; too long sunk in a sodden intellectual and spiritual torpor.

Their rulers, the magnificent caste of the Ayar-Incas, were the victims of their own power and luxury. So long accustomed to unlimited authority, they allowed Pizarro to advance to Cajamarca without serious concern. Atahualpa and his council undoubtedly knew of Pizarro's invasion of the emperor's authority on the coast,—his confiscation of lands and people,—and yet the Inca took no steps to stop or destroy the invader in the narrow mountain passes as he advanced into the heart of the country.

It seemed that some fatal illusion had fallen over the whole empire, from Inca to peasant slave, and paralyzed its defense. It would appear that for the lack of one single effort an empire and its culture fell,—which, had it stood, might have changed the course of civilization. If Atahualpa had strangled Pizarro instead of being strangled by him the mines of Potosí would not have filled the coffers of Charles I and Philip II.

The culture of the Andes, strengthened and not destroyed by contact with Europe, would have contributed much to the art and philosophy of the world. With all of its accomplishments,—far superior in many respects to the corresponding culture of Europe of that date,—the

[6] Prescott, *Conquest of Peru*, Vol. I, p. 371.

empire of the Incas perished in a contemptible struggle
because its people were slaves.[7]

[7] According to Dr. Justo Sahuaraura (*Monarquia Peruana*), Huayna
Ccapac had two sisters for wives. The first was sterile. The second bore
Huascar, who was murdered by his half-brother Atahualpa. Sahuaraura
claims that Atahualpa was an illegitimate son. It has been widely asserted
and accepted that Atahualpa's mother was a lady of Quito and that Atahualpa was born in that city. Sahuaraura states that Huayna Ccapac had a
third queen, a lady of Cuzco, Mama Runtu, his first cousin. She bore him
Manco Inca.

Sir Clements Markham (*Incas*, etc., p. 241, note) makes it quite clear
that Atahualpa was born in Cuzco and states that he "was a grown man
before he ever left Cuzco." Markham gives quite a different account, in
some respects, of Huayna Ccapac's family from that given by Sahuaraura.
He says that the conqueror emperor's "first queen was Mama Cusirimay,"
and that she was "the mother of his eldest son, Ninan Cuyuchi. The second
and favourite queen was Mama Rahua Ocllo, the mother of Inti Cusi
Hualpa, who was surnamed Huascar, from the village near Cuzco where he
was born. The third was named Tocta Cuca, a princess of the lineage of
Pachacuti, and the mother of Atahualpa. Mama Runtu was the fourth,
mother of the princes Manco and Paullu."

Ninan Cuyuchi was taken by Huayna Ccapac along with his other son,
Atahualpa, and Ninan's mother, Cusirimay, and Rahua (the mother of
Huascar and the Emperor's favorite queen) on his campaign of conquest
in the north, in which he was occupied for twelve years. Huayna Ccapac,
"the last of the imperial Incas," died at Quito in 1525 and his mummy
was brought to Cuzco and entombed there with great ceremony. (In view
of the common assumption that smallpox, a disease of Asiatic origin, did
not exist in America before the arrival of the Spaniards, Cúneo-Vidal's
statement, *Life of Pizarro*, p. 289, that Huayna Ccapac died of smallpox
is quite interesting.)

Huayna Ccapac, as death approached, made a declaration leaving the empire to his eldest son, Ninan Cuyuchi; and as the latter was in bad health
the Emperor nominated his second son, Huascar, to be Inca in case of his
elder brother's death. Ninan died very soon and Huascar was proclaimed
Emperor. Atahualpa made war on his brother, defeated his troops, took
him prisoner, and during his own incarceration by Pizarro in Cuzco, caused
Huascar to be drowned in the river Andamarca. Atahualpa himself was
betrayed, captured, and killed by Pizarro.

After the death of Atahualpa and Huascar, Pizarro "delivered the Incarial insignia to Tupac Cussi Huallpa . . . and invested him with the ap-
pearances, if not the reality, of imperial rule." (Rómulo Cúneo-Vidal,
Life of Francisco Pizarro, Barcelona, p. 289.) This prince is called
Toparca by Prescott, Tubalipa by other historians of the conquest. Vidal
quotes Juan Santa Cruz Pachacuti as saying that he was the "bastard son of
Huayna Ccapac," and the half-brother of Huascar and Atahualpa. He was

soon poisoned by Calcuchima, one of Atahualpa's generals, even though at the time Calcuchima himself was held a prisoner by Pizarro. It is said that Calcuchima gave the new Inca a slow poison in a cup of chicha (native beer).

Calcuchima was shortly afterwards charged by Pizarro with fomenting an insurrection against Pizarro's authority (a charge which, in view of Pizarro's position in the country, was almost comic in its audacity), and was shortly after burned at the stake.

Pizarro then allowed the Inca chiefs to place Manco, another son of Huayna Ccapac, upon the throne of the Inca. Manco's rule was a mere travesty under the control of the Spanish conquerors. Tiring of the humiliation he was subjected to, he retired to the wild mountain region of the Vilcapampa, lying to the north of Cuzco between the great gorges of the Urubamba and the Apurimac, where he lived amid the superb scenery and delightful climate of that lovely hill country in the middle or temperate zone between the warmth of the lowlands and the frozen heights. From thence he carried on a courageous and more or less successful guerrilla warfare against his Spanish oppressors. While he was playing at bowls one day with some low-class Spanish renegades whom he was entertaining, a quarrel arose and he was killed by one of the Spaniards.

This is the region of the more or less mythical Tampu-Tocco to which the remnants of the Ayar-Amautas and their followers fled after the defeat and death of their king, Pachacuti VI, in the Battle Gap of Vilcanota.

The authentic traditions list eighteen rulers of the archaic Pirua line. This dynasty was followed by forty-six kings of the Amautas (prophets, "wise men," and priests). When the invaders "from the south" had driven the last of them from their stronghold in the pass of La Raya and occupied the beautiful valley of Cuzco and the upper Vilcanota, the fugitives retired to the Vilcapampa. Here they nurtured the old religion of Viracocha and gradually reestablished the ancient Ayar discipline.

During this "dark age" the traditions which the Ayars preserved tell of twenty-one kings who ruled in Tampu-Tocco. During this period it is supposed they constructed, with the disciplined labor of their people, the city of refuge of Machu Picchu and the impregnable fortress of Salapunco at the narrows of the river.

From Tampu-Tocco, after this long period of obscurity, Ayar Manco emerged and reestablished the old religion and the Ayar rule in Cuzco. Seventeen Ayars, beginning with Ayar Manco, including the great conquering Emperors, Pachacuti and Tupac Yupanqui, and ending with Huascar, are listed in the *Inca* dynasty, though Rocca, the eighth in line from Ayar Manco, was the first to be called by that title.

It was to this same fastness of Vilcapampa, which had sheltered their fathers after the defeat of Pachacuti VI, that the last remnants of the Inca line fled from the Spanish invader. This time there was to be no renascence.

Sayri Tupac, the son of Manco, succeeded his father as Inca in Vilcapampa. Some time later, under offers of amnesty by the Spaniards, he came to Cuzco, but soon retired to his country-place in the beautiful valley of

Yucay, where he died shortly afterwards. Sahuaraura (*Monarquia Peruana*) intimates that Sayri was poisoned by order of the Spanish rulers.

Upon the death of Sayri his brother Titu Cusi Yupanqui assumed the title of Inca in Vilcapampa. Yupanqui was visited in his mountain fastness by Spanish priests sent by the Viceroy, Don Francisco de Toledo ("a younger son of the Count of Oropesa, belonging to a family of which the butcher Alva was the head." Markham calls him the "villain of the piece"). The mission was sent in the hopes of converting the Inca to Christianity and of receiving his submission. During the residence of the priests with him the Inca became sick and died. The Indians attributed his death to the incantations of the priest, Friar Ortiz, and killed the friar and his interpreter.

The chiefs then brought the Inca's younger brother, Tupac Amarú, then about twenty-five years of age, from the seclusion in which he had been kept through the jealousy of his elder brother, and put upon his brow the royal *borla*, or scarlet fringe. The imperial mantle was placed upon his shoulders and the bracelet upon his wrist. The Incarial parasol was held over him. He was given the golden battle-ax, the knife, lance, shield, and shoes of sovereignty. Then he was carried in the imperial litter and placed upon the throne. The royal headdress or crown (*masca-paycha*, shaped something like a Hindu turban, topped by two imperial feathers in front) was placed upon his head and reverence was done to him as the sovereign Inca. (Markham, *Incas*, etc., 292.)

Although the young monarch had had nothing whatever to do with the execution of the priests, as he was his brother's prisoner at the time this occurred, an expedition of soldiers was sent to capture him and he was brought to Cuzco and killed in the most cruel fashion under the orders of the Viceroy Toledo. His body was quartered and his head placed upon a pole in the public square.

It is related that in the dead hours of the night a noise as of the murmur of many voices was heard in the city and it was discovered that as by some spontaneous movement the people had come into the square and were on their knees doing reverence to the dissevered head of the last of the divine Sons of the Sun.

END OF VOLUME I